MW00435990

MONEY
BOSS MOM

MONEY BOSS MOM

HELPING YOUNG PARENTS BE THE "BOSS" OF THEIR FINANCIAL FUTURE

JAMIE A. BOSSE, CFP®

NEW DEGREE PRESS

COPYRIGHT © 2021 JAMIE A. BOSSE, CFP®
All rights reserved.

MONEY BOSS MOM
Helping Young Parents Be the "Boss" of Their Financial Future

ISBN   978-1-63676-741-3   *Paperback*
         978-1-63730-479-2   *Kindle Ebook*
         978-1-63730-480-8   *Ebook*

Dedication

To Weylan,

THANK YOU!

Thank you for loving me even when I am stressed out to the max.
Thank you for believing in me even when I stop believing in myself.
Thank you for supporting me when I embark on crazy adventures
like this one. I couldn't have done it without you. I love you.

To Oscar, Landry, Ellie, and Auggie,

You are my greatest achievement. Thank you for letting
mommy hide out in her office to complete this project. I love
you all so much, and I hope I make you proud someday.

To Baby B,

Even though we never got to meet you, know you are loved.

CONTENTS

INTRODUCTION 9

CHAPTER 1. MONEY IS A TOOL, NOT A GOAL 21
CHAPTER 2. BUILDING NET WORTH—
            THE FOUNDATION 39
CHAPTER 3. CASH FLOW—WHERE THE MAGIC
            HAPPENS 59
CHAPTER 4. INSURING YOUR BIGGEST ASSET—
            YOURSELF! 75
CHAPTER 5. ESTATE PLANNING—WHAT EVERY
            PARENT NEEDS TO KNOW 91
CHAPTER 6. THE RETIREMENT POGO STICK 109
CHAPTER 7. INVESTING SHOULD BE BORING 125
CHAPTER 8. COLLEGE FUNDING 149
CHAPTER 9. FOR THE LOVE—MONEY AND
            RELATIONSHIPS 163
CHAPTER 10. PREPARING FOR THE FINANCIAL IMPACT
            OF MATERNITY LEAVE AND RETURNING
            TO WORK WITH EASE 175
CHAPTER 11. TEACHING KIDS ABOUT MONEY WHEN IT
            IS INVISIBLE 187

CONCLUSION 209
ACKNOWLEDGMENTS 213
APPENDIX 219

INTRODUCTION

———

Picture this: Jake and Monica are in their mid-thirties with three small children. Monica is an engineer and Jake is a pharmacist, so they make good income and live in a beautiful home in a desirable school district. They are living the American Dream. Despite "having it all," they always feel like they are struggling. That big, beautiful house comes with a big, ugly mortgage. Their nice cars are expensive to service and insure and come with substantial monthly payments. Daycare is expensive, occasionally the credit card balance gets out of hand, and the graduate school loan is far from being paid off. They are educated, paid well, and doing "better" than average by any standard. Why isn't it enough?

It doesn't seem possible that they bring in a high six-figure income and still live paycheck to paycheck. They get pay increases and bonuses every year but have no extra money or savings to show for it. Jake and Monica are constantly asking themselves, "What are we doing wrong?" and "Why aren't we in a better place financially?" Without a cash cushion, they just can't afford to take any risks. Jake can't leave a job he hates for one that would energize him but pay less.

Monica wants to start her own business but is terrified to leave a steady paycheck, stock options, and health insurance benefits. They are constantly overwhelmed and just feel trapped.

The "American Dream" can become the American Nightmare before you realize it.

If you are reading this book, I assume you are already a parent or getting on the reproduction/adoption train soon. Presumably, folks in this baby-making stage are in Gen X, Gen Y (the millennials), or the very top end of Gen Z. Here are some definitions by Pew Research Center if you are not sure where you fall:

Generation X—Born 1965–1980
Millennials—Born 1981–1996
Generation Z—Born after 1996

I am in the millennial category—born in 1982, so you might refer to me as an "elder" millennial. I was around when movies had to be rewound, wearing seat belts in a moving car wasn't mandatory, and the internet only had one speed— dial-up. As a kid, I spent all my money on cassette tapes and Wild Pitch Watermelon Big-League Chew bubble gum. I didn't have a cell phone until I was in my twenties, and Facebook didn't exist until I was a full-blown adult. (If you are wondering what college life was like without broadcasting your every move on social media, it was glorious!) Even when I met my husband, many of our dates included a trip to Blockbuster Video to physically rent a movie to watch and then return the next day. *#OldSchool*

We millennials are in trouble. We have been dubbed the "unluckiest generation" by *The Atlantic* and *The Washington Post* because we just can't catch a break or get ahead. We are kids of crisis who have been impacted by market downturns more than any other generation. My fellow "elders" and I were in college or high school jamming to "Country Grammar" by Nelly in the early 2000s when the dot-com bubble burst and the Twin Towers fell, wreaking havoc on the economy. We were a few years into our careers and could finally afford our first iPhone when the Great Recession of 2008–2009 devastated the markets once again.

As people low on the totem pole, we were the first to lose our jobs when budgets were slashed or "restructuring" was required. I was working for a bank during the Great Recession and found myself on the chopping block along with millions of others across America. Recent college graduates had a hard time finding work, so they moved back in with their parents or went back to school to rack up more student loan debt. The "lucky ones" who did not lose their jobs saw no pay increases and had stagnant wages for years to come.

Things were good for a while, and then came the COVID-19 pandemic of 2020. This crisis cut deep in countless ways. From a financial standpoint, those in the service industry, small business owners, and "gig" workers suffered significantly. Many people in all generations were in the precarious position of not having a cash cushion going into the coronavirus shutdown.

During this particular pandemic, the Gen Xer's and millennial elders were likely married (or divorced) with mortgages,

minivan payments, and children to support. These generations have seen more than their fair share of disasters that
have stunted job prospects, professional growth, and earning
potential, but that's just part of the story. According to *Forbes*
(2019), millennials were leaving the nest right as the economy
and the landscape of higher education were shifting. During
our lifetimes, college costs have risen significantly, increasing
68 percent from 1999 to 2019.

Comedian Hasan Minhaj went before a congressional committee saying student loans have "put up a paywall to the
middle class." He shared some statistics based on the actual
prices the members of the committee paid for college thir-
ty-three years before. He noted, on average, the committee
had paid an inflation-adjusted $11,690 in tuition each year.
Tuition at those same schools in 2019 was nearly $25,000 a
year. That equates to a 110 percent increase in the cost of
tuition for college students in 2019, while wages had only
increased 16 percent over those thirty years. So, we graduate
from college with a degree and soul-crushing amounts of
debt during times of high unemployment, low wages, and
down markets. Nothing a little teamwork and a participation
ribbon won't fix.

These financial hardships are affecting more than just our
bank account balances. Dr. Galen Buckwalter is a psychologist who researches financial trauma and studies people's
relationships with money. He concluded one in four Americans have PTSD-like symptoms from financial stress. One in
four, you guys! Let that sink in. PTSD is a mental health condition triggered by a terrifying event—typically experiencing

it or witnessing it. How can our money be causing this debilitating level of distress?

Scott Saunders, CEO of Payoff (a financial wellness company), pointed to unbearably high debt levels, stagnant incomes, and nonexistent savings as potential issues that have contributed to this extreme level of stress. People who are in this state have significant problems at work, in social situations, and with relationships. It can impact their ability to function doing simple day-to-day tasks. Symptoms vary person to person but may include negative changes to thinking and mood, avoidance, nightmares, and physical and emotional reactions. In the study by Dr. Buckwalter in 2016, 23 percent of respondents were experiencing symptoms commonly associated with post-traumatic stress disorder because of financial stress. Among millennials, the number was over 35 percent. When our minds are trapped in a state of fear, it is impossible to think rationally and be able to plan and manage for the future.

With so much fear and anxiety about money, it is no wonder 66 percent of millennials have no savings for retirement (National Institute on Retirement Security, 2018). According to Pew Research Center, the median net worth of millennial households is about 40 percent lower than baby boomers and 17 percent less than Gen X at the same point in their lives (2019). These are startling statistics, and it doesn't have to be this way. Even though the younger generations have been shaped by financial adversity, it doesn't have to control the whole narrative of our lives.

I know this is starting to sound like a pity-party but hear me out. Sure, we can blame the economy, big banks, and helicopter parents for some of our problems, but there is a lot we can control. A common misperception is you must be born into money or earn a lot of money to be "wealthy," or you have to be a math whiz or a spreadsheet-lover to be "good with money."

It's not about how much money you make or how good you are at math. It's about the habits, systems, and behaviors you have that determine who is successful and who isn't, who is the boss of their financial future and who is a slave to their money. With the right systems in place, you can avoid a lot of stressful experiences in the first place. The financial trials you do face end up being much less traumatic. Financial setbacks become more of a nuisance instead of a full-blown emergency when you are ready for them.

This book will provide you with a tool kit that puts you in the driver's seat of your financial life. It will help you identify what is in your way and empower you to do something about it. As you embark on this journey to become a "Money Boss," you will find making a series of small shifts today will get you big results in the long run. It will help you discover the life you want to lead and show you how to use your money as a tool to get you there.

MY ONGOING JOURNEY

I grew up in a typical working-class household in the middle of Kansas. My mom worked in the deli at the grocery store, and my dad was a mechanic. I didn't really know anyone who "had money." All *those* people lived "on the hill" and went to the other high school, according to the rumors. Somehow, I concluded building wealth and having money to spare was actually a *bad* thing, like if you had extra money saved up, you must be selfish or greedy and don't deserve it.

My parents thought college was a big, scary place where good kids become alcoholics and white-collar pansies who didn't know how to change a tire. I decided to go to college anyway and was the first one in my family to do so. There was no college fund or savings account for me, so I applied for every scholarship I could and accepted any loan amount they would give me. I worked as a waitress to supplement my borrowed income from Sallie Mae.

When I was a sophomore in college, my mom called to tell me my parents were filing for bankruptcy. *Bankruptcy?* A million thoughts buzzed around in my head: *Will they be homeless? Are they going to jail? Am I going to have to drop out of school to raise my siblings? How did this happen? What does it mean?*

At this point in my young adult life, I already had three credit cards, zero savings, and a rapidly growing student loan debt balance. I had to figure out how to prevent this from happening to me, and I knew I had a lot to learn. So, I signed up to take Personal Finance 101 at Kansas State University the very next semester. I was fascinated by the topics and realized helping people navigate their financial lives could be an incredibly rewarding career. I changed my major to Personal Financial Planning, became a Certified Financial

Planner®, and have been in the industry ever since. I have worked in different types of settings—a single advisor firm, a large private bank, and a mid-size independent advisory firm.

My story could have easily gone the same way my parents' story did, but I empowered myself with education to change that trajectory. I have battled through paying off credit cards and experienced low wages and job loss while trying to make a dent in my student loan balance. I have studied and experimented with multiple ways of managing cash flow and merging finances to find one that works for my family and my clients. It has been a long and bumpy road, but I have gone from having a dangerously negative net worth to proactively building the financial future I desire for my family.

I am in this financial planning/parenting vortex with you. As I write this, I am a thirty-eight-year-old working mother of four. My husband and I are balancing the competing priorities of saving for retirement, planning for education costs, managing our careers, and handling the expenses of today. Those of you with kids ages five and under know daycare is like a second mortgage (and once you have more than one kid in care, it's probably more than your mortgage). I know what you are going through; I see you. I want to help you take control so you can be a "Money Boss" for your family.

THIS BOOK IS FOR YOU IF YOU ARE ANY OF THE FOLLOWING:

- A new parent or soon-to-be parent who wants help navigating this exciting, special, and terrifying phase of life.

- Parents in your twenties, thirties, or forties who want to gain control of your finances and protect those you love.
- Wanting to live well today but also plan for the future.
- Choosing to be proactive, not reactive, with your money and your time.
- Wanting to organize your financial life and break out of the paycheck-to-paycheck lifestyle.
- Going through a transition, like a change in marital status, a change in your job or career track, starting a business, buying or upgrading your home, and many others.
- An aspiring Money Boss.

WHAT YOU'LL LEARN

Money Boss Mom is designed to cover a variety of topics that lead to a healthy financial lifestyle. It is laid out in a nonlinear way, meaning you can skip around and read it out of order if you want to. You're busy, I know. If you have littles in the house, you're not even getting to sleep through the night, let alone have many quiet moments for peaceful, productive reading sessions. Use this book to educate yourself on the areas you haven't addressed yet or the things you struggle with. You can also use it to improve the things you already do well. Of course, I recommend you work with a Certified Financial Planner® Professional to address your specific goals and situation. There are a lot of common themes for this stage of life, but everyone's journey is different.

We will explore how to identify your unconscious bias about money, giving you important insights on *why* you manage money the way you do. This will give you the tools and knowledge to change that perspective and do something about it. When you understand your *why*, you can put an end to those bad habits and start to develop new ones that match the life you want to lead.

Parenthood comes with a lot of moving parts. This book covers how to manage the competing priorities of managing your career and saving for long-term goals, like retirement and education funding, while managing the expenses and demands of today. We will talk about the keys to getting cash flow under control and making your money work for you instead of the other way around. You will learn how to get the right systems in place for saving, investing, and handling emergencies so you can break the exhausting paycheck to paycheck lifestyle. You'll stop worrying so much about money because you'll know you're making the right decisions and are on track for success.

This will not be a lecture on what you should or shouldn't be doing with your money. I'm not going to beat you up about your past mistakes, where you are today, or how many lattes you buy in a week. I will provide some helpful tips and guidelines to get you on the trajectory to where to you want to be and *who* you want to be going forward.

Adulting is hard. Parenthood takes adulting to a whole other level. Not only are you responsible for paying bills on time, changing batteries in the smoke detectors, and unclogging the drain, but also you must now keep tiny humans safe, entertained, educated, and alive. Not to mention there is the task of raising them to be responsible adults. If you are experiencing issues with cash flow, debt, or any other financial insecurity, that is all you can think about. It will consume you. You are in fight or flight mode and can't focus on the ones you love most; you're just trying to make things work until the next paycheck. I want to help you take control of your money so you are confident you are doing the right things and are set up for a bright future.

It's time to get unstuck. It's time to be the boss of your financial future.

CHAPTER 1

MONEY IS A TOOL, NOT A GOAL

---

*"You do not rise to the level of your goals.
You fall to the level of your systems."*

—JAMES CLEAR, AUTHOR OF ATOMIC HABITS

*Moola, dinero, Benjamins, bacon, cheddar, bones, dough,
Gouda, paper, dollar dollar bills, y'all!*

Whether you refer to money as dead presidents, catchy phrases from '90s rap songs, or random forms of cheese, it is important to all of us.

Money itself is not good or bad; it is simply a means to an end, a tool to get what you need and do what you want. Most of the time your goal isn't *"I want more money."* It's *"I want more money so I can...(fill in the blank)."* Maybe you want to save up to take your son to Disney World for his seventh birthday. Maybe you want to be able to retire at fifty-five and travel across the country in an Airstream Flying Cloud. Maybe you want your kids to graduate college free of student loans because you have felt trapped by debt for most of your adult life. Money should be used to live the life you want.

"Money is a resource. It's not good, it's not bad, it's not evil, it's just a resource."
—FARNOOSH TORABI, CREATOR AND HOST OF SO MONEY

How we spend our money is determined by a combination of our habits, goals, and values, and those three things are not always in alignment. In this chapter, we will explore the reasons we handle money the way we do and how to distance ourselves from negative financial behaviors. We will explore why change is so hard and how we can start developing some positive habits with money to get closer to the lives we envision for ourselves.

MONEY SCRIPTS®

Money Status, Money Avoidance, Money Worship, Money Vigilance

Some of our habits around money stem all the way back from our childhood (Klontz 2011). These are what financial psychologist Brad Klontz refers to as "Money Scripts®." They are the unconscious money beliefs that drive our thinking, decisions, and reactions related to money. Klontz and his team have identified four different Money Scripts®—Money Status, Money Avoidance, Money Worship, and Money Vigilance.

You can exhibit characteristics in several or all categories but likely lean toward one or a couple of them. Here is a description of each and some tips on how to flip the script to your advantage.

MONEY STATUS

Those who fall in the Money Status category tend to link their self-worth to their net worth. They desperately try to "Keep up with the Joneses" and may be trying to maintain a lifestyle they simply can't afford. Klontz says they may have come from a household that gave a higher social standing to those people who had more money. Money Status seekers are prone to overspending, attracted to gambling, and may be guilty of hiding their purchases from their spouse.

FLIP THE SCRIPT—TIPS FOR MONEY STATUS CHASERS

Know that money and your net worth does not define you. It is totally normal to want the latest and greatest stuff, but if you cannot afford it, you are hurting your family and your future. Klontz recommends asking yourself these questions before making a purchase:

- Why am I buying this item?
- Will it make me happy? For how long?
- How will I pay for it?
- Fast forward to a week from now. Does this purchase still make me happy?

Start discussing your spending honestly with your spouse and maybe a professional financial advisor. Focus on being deliberate with your spending by purchasing things that are important to you, not what you think will impress someone else.

MONEY AVOIDANCE

Those who show traits of Money Avoidance have an implied belief money is bad or corrupt. They assume those with a lot of money have a lower moral compass and don't deserve it. Money Avoiders tend to sabotage their financial success by giving money away, overspending, or ignoring their finances altogether.

FLIP THE SCRIPT—TIPS FOR MONEY AVOIDERS

Avoiding your money can be very dangerous. Make sure to at least check in with your financial situation once a month, even if it feels daunting. You can try to make it less threatening by making it a fun, pizza-and-wine dinner date with your spouse. Klontz recommends thinking of all the ways you can do good or benefit the world with money. Maybe you could start allocating some of your income to a charity you care about; that way, having money to give does not feel so negative.

MONEY WORSHIP

Money Worshippers believe money will solve all their problems and having money is the key to being happy. These are the emotional shoppers who buy new things simply because they think it will make them feel better. Money Worshippers often have trouble with credit card debt and might put work before family to generate more money.

FLIP THE SCRIPT—TIPS FOR MONEY WORSHIPPERS

Know your happiness is independent of what you have in the bank, how big your house is, or the possessions you own. This one is tricky because we are constantly bombarded on social media with all the cool things everyone has and is doing. Klontz recommends making a plan to give to an organization or cause that inspires you to offset the negative effects of Money Worship. Identify some of your buying habits. If you find you are often riddled with buyer's remorse, put some space between you and the next purchase. When you find something you want to buy, wait twenty-four hours and see if it is still appealing to you then.

MONEY VIGILANCE

Those in the Money Vigilant category are careful, watchful, and attentive to their financial health. They like bargains, hate debt, and typically live well within their means. They value working for their money and do not want any financial handouts. The Vigilant are good at saving and being frugal, sometimes to a fault. They may have a hard time spending and enjoying the money they have saved because they are anxious and overly worried.

FLIP THE SCRIPT—TIPS FOR THE MONEY VIGILANT

Klontz recommends people in this category should adopt the mindset of "Work hard, play hard." Continue to work hard and save but let yourself have a little fun too! He suggests earmarking a bucket of money purely as "fun money" for vacations, experiences, or indulgent purchases. These folks do well working with a financial planner because they can outsource some of their worrying to a professional.

Can you tell which Money Script® you relate to most? At the end of this chapter, there is a link to the assessment you can take to find out where you fall. It consists of thirty-two statements you rate, and it will let you know which Money Scripts® apply to you. If you want to make meaningful change and progress with your financial life, it is helpful to know where you're starting from.

WHY IS CHANGE SO HARD?

THE ELEPHANT AND THE RIDER

Chip and Dan Heath, authors of *Switch: How to Change Things When Change Is Hard,* believe making positive changes requires redirection through motivation. They build on the analogy by psychologist Jonathan Haidt which states there are two sides to human nature—the rider and the elephant. Picture a person literally riding an elephant. (I have done this in real life, by the way, and it is not as cool as it looks. It's great for a photo op, but the hair of an elephant is like pokey wires jabbing your legs, and it's a pretty bumpy ride). The rider is the logical side—the rational thinker who makes decisions based on facts and evidence through analysis. The elephant is the emotional side—characterized by intuition, sympathy, and loyalty. Based on instincts or gut feelings, the elephant may refuse to move, back away, or rear up. The elephant prefers quick gratification over long-term thinking and is often on autopilot.

You know that feeling when you are driving to work in the morning and you don't actually remember the drive, parking the car, or stopping at all the traffic lights? That is your inner elephant taking over. You completely zone out and get there without having to think about it. This is because you've done it so many times that the drive has become a habit. Habits help us get through the day by making some of our tasks relatively effortless. Our brains love going into autopilot—no thinking, no feeling, just chugging along. We subconsciously revert to the easiest way to do something; we are wired to take the path of least resistance (Psychology Today 2017). Therefore, changing a habit that is already ingrained is really hard to do. Think about it. You hear people say things like this all the time: "I need to quit smoking," "I need to exercise," and, of course, "I need to save money." Yet they do nothing about it. Why? Because it is so much easier to just continue their normal routine and not try to reroute their elephant.

Since the rider has the reins, you get the sense the rider is in charge, like he or she is leading or guiding the elephant. Here's the thing—the elephant does what she wants (driven by emotion—remember?), and a tiny little rider won't be able to stop her. The elephant part of the brain may tell us to go ahead and eat the whole sleeve of Girl Scout Cookies after the rider has already decided we are starting our New Year's diet. The rationale of making smart financial decisions appeals to the rider in all of us. Spending less than we make, saving for the long term, and being prepared for emergencies all make logical sense to our inner rider. But the elephant in us is just worried about what feels good right now, not the long-term game. Right now, a new pair of shoes, a bigger TV, or a trip to Cabo sound like *way* more fun than saving money.

We must get our rider and our elephant in sync. Our emotional elephant side is not the enemy. It is part of who we are. We need goals and targets that appeal to both the rational *and* emotional sides of the coin.

Let's say you fall in the Money Status Seeker category from the Money Scripts® above. If you cut back spending because you think you "should," the elephant won't go for that. You will just fall back into your current routines of spending money throughout the day as you always have. In contrast, if you decide to make some cuts to spending to save up for a family vacation to Disney next year, that is something fun your elephant can get behind. Emotion gets involved. You can picture your daughter's smiling face when she meets Moana in person. You can feel your son's nervous excitement as he sees a real-life stormtrooper walk by. You get the warm-fuzzies just thinking about creating these amazing memories with your kids. Spending time with your family and having fun together is something you value, and it triggers an emotional response. When you cut back spending to make room for a bigger goal, giving up something you're doing now that is less important is not as painful.

START WITH THE OUTCOME

When thinking about your financial life, start with the end game in mind. What would you say if someone asked you, "What's the most important piece of a puzzle?" Some people say, "Duh, the corner pieces," while others think the first piece or the last piece are the way to go. Some deep thinkers may say something like, "All the pieces are equally important because if even one is missing, the puzzle is incomplete." Those answers are great, but the real answer is the picture on the box. The picture on the box provides vision and clarity so you can see what you are striving for and trying to create. This is the most important piece of the puzzle. With the bigger picture in mind, you can start to see how all the smaller pieces need to line up.

When I meet with new clients, I often ask them a question along these lines:

"Say we are sitting at this table three years from now. What would have happened between now and then for you to feel like this relationship was worth it?"

The responses vary widely, but there are usually a few things top of mind. Maybe it's a desire to pay off all their debts outside the mortgage, to upgrade to a larger house before the next baby comes, or to figure out how to live on one income so one partner can pursue a dream that involves a pay cut. Maybe they feel out of control and just want to feel like they have a plan. Once we figure out what three years from now looks like, we can devise a system to get there, starting now. With most clients, the sooner they define a goal and start working on it, the sooner they will get to where they want to be.

Think about where you want to be and *who* you want to be in three years, in five years, in twenty years, and work backward from there.

My husband and I both grew up in Kansas and then moved away to other states after college. He started out in Illinois and then moved to Texas, where we met and started dating. A few years later, he was offered a job opportunity in Portland, Oregon. We had never been to the West Coast, so we thought, "Why not?" We moved to Oregon and lived there for seven years before moving back to Kansas to settle in. I love that we traveled around and that living in different states is a part of our story. We have four kids, and I hope their adventures take them to other states and countries along the way. My big goal in retirement is to be comfortable enough financially that I can always travel to see my kids, no matter where they live, without cost being an issue. Of course, it's tempting to ignore the long term and spend more money on all kinds of stuff now, but when I think about the big picture, I would rather sock away more for retirement so I can make that dream a reality.

Having a vision for the future that is tied to your values is the key to making good financial decisions today.

In my discussions with Amy Mullen, CFP®, president of Money Quotient, Inc., I found the "vision" is where you get the inspiration to make changes and implement healthy financial behaviors. She says, "When you can really envision what a fulfilling and meaningful life looks like for you, it becomes a lot easier to frame your decisions around what is going to bring you closer to that vision and what will push you further from it."

On a podcast with financial guru Michael Kitces, Amy gives the example of the typical weight loss goal: "Here's how that conversation usually goes: 'I should work out four times a week. I should stop eating sugar. I should, I should, I should…'" All these "shoulds" don't inspire any action. They just make you feel bad about yourself. Amy instead suggests, "Describe what it would be like if you were already living your best life. Make it visceral. What does it look like? What does it sound like? How does it make you feel?" The difference with the weight loss goal might sound like, "I am feeling healthy and strong. When my friends ask if I want to go hiking this weekend, I enthusiastically say yes because I know I can keep up! I enjoy playing soccer with my grandson and don't get winded."

The vision of playing soccer with your grandson makes the goal of working out and eating better more meaningful. Now apply this in the financial sense. The goal really isn't "I need to save more so I can retire." It's "I want to have enough money in retirement so I can X…" Amy says, "Retirement is just a word. If it doesn't have a vision behind it, you're just looking at numbers."

"When you are able to create a compelling vision of something you really want, suddenly the steps to getting there don't feel quite so painful."

—AMY N. MULLEN, CFP®, PRESIDENT

OF MONEY QUOTIENT, INC.

THE POWER OF HABITS

Now that you see how your goals and values play into the big picture vision, you must figure out how to get all the puzzle pieces in place to make it happen. Having a goal isn't enough. It's not just about the big decisions you make; it's also what you do every day that matters. James Clear, the author of *Atomic Habits,* says, "If you get just 1 percent better each day for a year, you'll end up 37 times better by the time you're done." Habits can compound for or against you. Let's go back to the example of a weight loss goal. You typically don't just lose a bunch of weight quickly by making one change. You lose weight over time by making small changes to your sleep habits, calorie intake, and exercise program. Making little tweaks in a positive direction makes a big difference over time.

The same principles apply to financial goals. Let's say you have $1,000 in a Roth IRA today. If you start contributing fifty dollars a month to it now, that may not seem like a big enough shift to make a significant difference. However, if you keep up that small habit for twenty years, you could end up with $30,085 in that Roth IRA (assuming a 7 percent rate of return). So, you end up putting in $12,000 over that time frame, and the magic of compound interest and returns does the rest.

The compounding power of habits (or interest) can always work against you as well. Think about when you have one of those days where nothing seems to go right. You stub your toe in the morning, then you miss a deadline at work, then your jerk coworker takes credit for your project in a meeting, then your husband forgets to pick up the dog, then your kids spill glue all over the carpet. Each of those items is mildly stressful, but when you add them all together, you have had one terrible day!

Negative financial habits can build up as well.

Marla mindlessly charges small purchases on her credit card here and there throughout the day. At the end of the month, she looks at her statement and is baffled by the huge balance. All those small purchases add up to a big number, then the credit card company adds 16 percent in interest, so she feels like she can never get ahead.

Kevin has a habit of stopping at the QuikTrip every morning before work. He knows he'd be better off making his own coffee and bringing snacks from home, but it's just so handy to stop in there on his way. Kevin ends up buying his morning coffee, his afternoon snacks, and a *Bahama Breeze* air freshener on today's visit. If he does this every morning, that eleven dollars a day, five days a week adds up to $220 spent a month on stuff that maybe isn't that important to him.

ADDRESS THE GOAL AND THE SYSTEM

Actress Debi Mazar is quoted as saying, "The kitchen is the heart of every home." I think she is right. My family spends a lot of time in the kitchen, and any time we have guests over, everyone seems to congregate there—specifically around the island. Picture this: a simple but gorgeous vase of farm-cut flowers atop a clean, sparkly, clutter-free kitchen island where everyone can gather in perfect harmony. You feel a warm, minimalist, Joanna Gaines-type vibe, right? Can you see it?

Well, that's not my house. In real life, if the kitchen is the heart of every home, mine is suffering from a cardiac arrest—code blue. My kitchen island is a wasteland of abandoned mail, children's artwork, half-eaten Clif Bars, mismatched Tupperware lids, and the occasional snow cone machine. I clean that thing off at least once a week or any time someone is coming over. So, I essentially accomplish the *goal* of getting it cleaned up, but I've done nothing to address the system that makes it cluttered in the first place. I leave sticky note reminders there and unload the daycare bags there. The kids unload their backpacks on it each day. All the minimalist folks have a different system in place to keep areas like that clean. Mail is looked through and discarded or put in a specific place for processing later. Backpacks have a place that is not located in a high-traffic area. The snow cone machine has a home in a cupboard somewhere. I must change my system if I want to reach the goal.

My friend Christyn is a prime example of someone who keeps her house in amazing shape. I bet she doesn't have to shove a bunch of stuff in a closet every time someone comes over because everything has its place and is already where it belongs. If I were to make a surprise visit to her house right now, I guarantee I would find her naked countertops in immaculate condition with just a lovely bouquet on display. Sometimes, when I catch myself piling stuff up on the counter, I ask myself, "What would Christyn do?"

When it comes to your financial systems, think of someone you know who is doing things the way you wish you did and ask yourself, "What would they do right now if they were me?" Maybe it's a real person, or maybe it's just a version of yourself you can envision. Start thinking like the person you want to become.

OUTSMART YOUR ELEPHANT

Remember Marla, who shops mindlessly, and Kevin, the QuikTripper, from the example above? If you have some similar vices, here are some tips on how you could beat those ingrained habits and start new ones.

If you are the like Marla and frequent, small purchases get out of control by the end of the month, identify the cues that spark this habit. Maybe you work in a cool downtown area that has a million shops around. You go on a walk every day over the lunch hour to be healthy and get some fresh air. On your walks this week, you stopped in at Nordstrom Rack, Macy's, and Carter's and bought around $600 worth of items you didn't actually need. The walk is a healthy habit, but your elephant is conditioned to want to shop every time you walk by these retail havens. You must find a way to trick your elephant to change its reaction. Next week, go on a walk without your wallet or your phone. That way, if you are tempted to buy something, you can't. You'll be forced to go back to the office without an armful of new items. Once you've had the afternoon to think about it, you can decide if you want to journey back to those stores to make a purchase. Better yet, don't go into any stores at all on your walk unless there is something specific you need to pick up. Train yourself to call a friend when you're on the walk so you keep walking and talking instead of mindlessly shopping. Ask a coworker to join you and enjoy their company instead of drooling over the window displays as you walk by.

Kevin the QuikTripper could start shifting his habits to tame his elephant as well. He could start a new cue of leaving a portable coffee cup out in the morning, so he fills it up on his way out. He could load up his passenger seat with beef jerky and Cracker Jacks each night before work, so he feels ready for the day's snacking needs. Kevin could start phoning a friend on his drive, so he keeps talking instead of getting the urge to stop in. He could limit his QuikTrip visit to once a week or take a different route to work altogether.

Arm yourself with information. Start by identifying your ingrained behaviors, habits, and systems. Figure out your Money Script, your values, and your elephant's emotional tendencies. Once you know yourself better, you will be aware of your triggers and when you're stuck going down an old, familiar path. You can then outsmart the negative behaviors of your elephant by making small tweaks to your day.

"Whatever you have to do to gain self-knowledge, do it. Find out who you are and what you want. Then you can stop wasting your life energy and your money on stuff that doesn't matter to you—and start making financial decisions that will get you to your true goals."

—CARL RICHARDS, THE BEHAVIOR GAP

Don't beat yourself up about where you are today. Focus on getting on the right trajectory to where you want to be. If you start making small changes to your systems, you will start to see big results over the long run. In the next chapter, we will discuss some ways to build a strong financial foundation and make meaningful changes to grow your net worth (increase assets, decrease liabilities).

"MONEY BOSS" SYSTEMS FOR SUCCESS—CHAPTER 1

- Discover your Money Scripts® by taking the assessment at www.yourmentalwealthadvisors.com.
- Identify your habits and behaviors around money and which ones you'd like to change.
- Create a vision for the financial life you want to lead and the person you want to become.
- Make small tweaks to your day to change these habits and ingrained negative behaviors.

CHAPTER 2

BUILDING NET WORTH— THE FOUNDATION

———

"What determines your wealth is not how much you make, but how much you keep."

—DAVID BACH

First, what is net worth and why does it matter? Your net worth is your assets minus your liabilities.

ASSETS – LIABILITIES = NET WORTH

Everything you *own* minus everything you *owe* equals your net worth. This is sometimes referred to as your "balance sheet." The asset side of the equation can include anything of monetary value: bank account balances, your house, retirement accounts, vehicles, equipment, etc. The liability side might include your mortgage, car loans, credit cards, and student debt. Many younger adults and recent graduates actually have a *negative* net worth because they owe more in student loans than they own in assets. In that situation, it is okay to have a negative net worth, but you want to make sure you are taking steps to get to the positive side. Net worth is basically a snapshot of your overall financial health at a specific moment in time. It is important to track it each year to ensure your wealth is moving in the right direction. As you pay down debt and build your retirement nest egg, that number should grow.

Consistently increasing your net worth over time is the foundation of building true wealth. I am not talking about wealth in terms of Elon Musk, Oprah, or other icons we affiliate with "being wealthy" or having an astronomically high net worth. I am talking about wealth in the sense of *freedom.* When you have a strong and growing net worth, you have the flexibility to create the life you want for yourself. You are no longer a slave to the paycheck-to-paycheck lifestyle or "working for the man." You get to the point where you are working because you choose to, not because you "have" to. You are living life on your terms, not someone else's.

"Think of your net worth like a battleship during a time of war. As the intrepid captain, you are navigating your net worth to glory through sea mines of temptation and unknown icebergs of economic downturns. The greater you build your net worth, the more careful you steer."
— THE FINANCIAL SAMURAI

Net worth is a gauge of your financial health, but it doesn't tell the whole story. It's kind of like your body weight; it matters, but you need more info to determine if that number is healthy. With body weight, you must look at other factors, like height, muscle mass, bone structure, blood pressure, cholesterol, etc., to know if you are in overall good shape. Net worth is the same. You must consider your age, income, spending level, where you live (e.g., the cost of living in Manhattan, New York is very different than that of Manhattan, Kansas), and what assets make up that net worth. If you have one million dollars in net worth, but it is all in real estate, and you have no cash for emergencies, you are not financially healthy.

Key components on the asset side include the following:

- Cash
- Retirement assets
- Physical assets
- Taxable assets (investments in non-retirement accounts)

Here's what to focus on in each of these areas and why:

ASSET COMPONENT #1—THE IMPORTANCE OF CASH

It was Friday, February 15, 2019, just after Valentine's Day. We were lame, exhausted parents and didn't make any big plans for the evening or the weekend. At the time, our two oldest kids were ages five and four, and our infant twins would celebrate their first birthday in a couple of days. My husband, Weylan, had an afternoon call scheduled with his manager.

Here's a pro tip: Friday afternoon calls with management are *always* a red flag, my friends. As you have already guessed, Weylan was being let go from his job.

A forced change in employment is always an unsettling experience, but when you are a parent, it is especially nerve-racking. Weylan's income was almost double what mine was, so depending on how long this stint of unemployment lasted, we would most certainly have to dip into savings to cover expenses. There were of course things that could be cut—eating out, clothing purchases, entertainment, etc.—but the mortgage payment, daycare tuition (which was more than twice our mortgage payment at the time), car payment, and other monthly bills would stay the same. Of course, we had an emergency fund prepared for just this kind of catastrophe. A fully funded emergency stash should be about three to six months' worth of your fixed expenses (the stuff you must pay). Admittedly, ours was closer to the three-month mark than the six-month target.

According to Indeed.com, the average amount of time it takes to find a job is about nine weeks. The more money you earn and the more specific the position you would accept, the longer it takes to find a good fit. There is a well-known saying that you can expect your job search to take one month for every $10,000 you are going to earn. So, if you're applying for jobs that pay $50,000, you can expect it to take approximately five months to find a job. If you're looking in the $100,000 range, expect it to take up to ten months (Career Sidekick 2020). If you are well connected in your industry and have your LinkedIn page and resume up to date, that will likely shorten the timeline. If you consider all the internal processes that happen within companies (talking to recruiters, reviewing resumes, first interviews, second interviews, formulating the offer, etc.), the process will take at least three months.

Weylan ended up in a new position that he was excited about in July of 2019. So, that was about a four-and-a-half to five-month unemployment process for us. We made it through relatively unscathed but wished we had saved a six-month emergency fund at the start of that whole mess.

Not having an emergency fund is one of the biggest landmines young parents come up against. When you do not have enough cash on hand to cover a couple months of no income, the refrigerator going out, or an unexpected emergency room bill, your cash flow will be derailed for months, and it's hard to get back on track. When you must find cash fast, you either run up a credit card bill, borrow it from someone, or take it from somewhere you shouldn't—like your 401(k). Then, you must pay that back or deal with the tax damage from taking a premature retirement withdrawal. According to the Federal Reserve (2018), 47 percent of Americans could not even come up with $400 in the case of an emergency. This is a scary position to be in because the "unexpected" is just a part of life—especially when you are a homeowner and have kids. A family of squirrels burrow into your siding, water heaters need to be replaced, windows get broken, toddlers jam random items into their noses or ears—you get the picture. Expect to pay at least 1 percent of the home's value every year in maintenance-related costs, and remember—parenting is full of emergencies!

Side note: cash is *not* always king. Think of it more like a knight—coming to your rescue in shining armor, of course). As with everything in life, moderation is key. There is such a thing as having too much cash. If you are hoarding cash and not investing because you fear the market, you may actually be losing money by keeping it on the sidelines. Cash piled up under the mattress will not keep up with the cost of living or inflation. You know when you buy a stamp for fifty-five cents and your grandpa shakes his fist and declares, "I remember when stamps cost a nickel!"? It's the same principal here. The cost of everything you buy will likely increase, so some of your money needs to be invested to outpace inflation in the long-term. Have at least three months' worth of spending needs in cash. At maximum, have emergency funds of up to twelve to twenty-four months' worth of spending needs in cash. (Caveat—if you are currently saving for a down payment or other large purchase in cash, it's okay to have your emergency fund plus enough cash for whatever it is you are saving for.) No emergency fund yet? Here are some tips to get started:

THREE "MONEY BOSS" TIPS FOR BUILDING AN EMERGENCY FUND

1. Automate:

People tend to spend whatever is in their checking account, so put it somewhere else from the start. Remember the rider and the elephant analogy from chapter one? If your elephant side doesn't like to save, make saving automatic so you don't actually have to do anything. Have a portion of your paycheck directly deposited into a separate savings account that you have earmarked for emergencies only and try not to look at it very often. Once you have this system in place for a while, you'll be used to the amount you *can* spend each month. Remember, you should aim to always have three to six months' worth of your fixed expenses available in an emergency fund. Once you reach that amount, you can move the direct deposit to another account to pay off debt, save for other goals, or to invest.

2. Hide it from yourself:

Out of sight, out of mind. It is easier to build funds if you are not constantly tempted to use them. If your elephant is an emotional spender, do not give it access to the funds in the first place! Do not keep your emergency fund in the same bank you use for daily expenditures. Better yet, utilize an online bank so you cannot see the balance in your normal bank login. As a bonus, accounts at these banks will often earn a higher interest rate than those at brick-and-mortar banks. If it must stay in cash, it might as well be earning something.

3. Take baby steps:

Building up a balance in any type of account takes time. Be patient with yourself and start slowly. If you currently live paycheck to paycheck (as 78 percent of Americans do, according to *Forbes*), finding "extra funds" can be difficult. Start looking for small ways to save a few dollars each week. You could skip the Starbucks run once a week and allocate that four dollars to savings or cancel a subscription that you rarely use. Begin redirecting a small amount of funds directly from your paycheck, even if it's just twenty-five dollars a pay period, and gradually increase it. Also, look for ways to capture "windfall" dollars that are in addition to your regular salary. Any time you receive a bonus, a gift of cash, or a tax refund, automatically put at least 10 percent of it into savings. When you get a raise at work, don't spend that extra amount each pay period; instead, redirect it toward building that emergency cushion.

Use these three tips to build your rainy-day fund and remember to only tap into it in the case of a *real* emergency. "Christmas is NOT an emergency!" In the words of Dave Ramsey, "It happens on the same day each year." Other non-emergencies include summer camp, college, weddings, and spontaneous shopping sprees. If you continually dip into these funds for non-emergencies, the funds will not be there when you really need them.

ASSET COMPONENT #2—PHYSICAL ASSETS

The physical asset category is exactly what you think it is. These include real estate—your house, vacation house, rental properties, farmland and equipment, cars, jewelry, and other items of sellable value. This is a tricky category because while these things have value and can be sold for cash, it is not always easy to do. If you or your spouse lose a job next Valentine's Day, you can't just sell your house or car to get the cash you need to make it through the next few months.

It is important not to be House-Poor, meaning your house has a lot of value, but you spend most of your income on it in the form of mortgage payments, insurance, property taxes, maintenance, and utilities. Out of your total net worth, your house should only be about 25 to 40 percent of that value (50 percent on the very top end—Financial Samurai). As the retirement and investment assets grow in your portfolio, the percentage of your overall net worth that is in real estate should decline. For instance, if you are thirty, it's totally fine for your home value to equal 40 percent of your net worth. When you're forty, it should be closer to 25 to 35 percent of the whole pie.

ASSET COMPONENT #3—RETIREMENT ASSETS

These are your long-term investments specifically earmarked for retirement. These usually take the form of company retirement plans like 401(k)s, 403(b)s, 457 plans, Thrift Savings Plans, SIMPLE IRAS, and pensions, or self-directed accounts, like traditional IRAs, Roth IRAs, and SEP IRAs. Retirement assets are generally the easiest buckets to build because most employers *force* you to make the savings automatic. You set up the percentage, and then the funds come out of your paycheck before you even see them—*brilliant!* Many employers allow you to increase the savings percentage automatically each year, so you don't even have to lift a finger to start saving more. You should target to save 10 to 15 percent of your income in the retirement savings bucket. This is just a teaser—all of chapter six is about retirement savings, so stay tuned for more on this topic.

ASSET COMPONENT #4—TAXABLE ASSETS: INVESTMENTS IN THE NON-RETIREMENT BUCKET

This is the bucket that is generally the hardest to build up. Many young parents seem to zone in on home ownership first, then start building the retirement bucket through company retirement plans, then focus on the emergency fund, so this one comes last. This is the freedom and flexibility bucket. As I mentioned before, physical assets—like a home—have value, but it's not value that you can use to pay bills or buy things. The retirement bucket is important to grow, but those assets generally cannot be touched without penalty until the age of fifty-nine and a half, so they are technically illiquid as well. We already discussed the importance of the emergency fund, but those funds are reserved for emergencies only. The taxable asset bucket is essentially funds that are invested and growing for you which do not have the restrictions of a retirement account.

This bucket can be used for spending needs if you retire early—before fifty-nine and a half when you can't access your IRA or 401(k) plan. You can invest funds in this bucket and use it to buy a second house in ten years, start a business down the road, or fund other goals. Here's an important note: if you anticipate using/needing these funds in the next twelve to twenty-four months, it is probably best to keep them in cash-like assets instead of investments as investment values fluctuate.

NOTE ON ALTERNATIVE ASSETS

There are many other assets that one can own as a part of their net worth. These can include cryptocurrency, fine arts, collectibles, silver or gold, etc. I chose not to dedicate much space to these assets because they are not the core building blocks of wealth and a strong net worth. They can have a place on your balance sheet but should be no more than 5 to 10 percent of your investable assets. Focus on building the four core asset component categories first, and then consider dabbling in alternatives if you have an interest in those areas.

THE LIABILITY SIDE OF THE NET WORTH EQUATION

Debt is the controversial side of the balance sheet, and rightfully so. Liabilities can add up fast, gobble up your income, and get you into trouble if you're not careful.

The most important part of the liability side of your net worth is that you know what your debts are and what they are costing you. Make a list of everything you owe and what the interest rate associated with that debt is. Typically, mortgages, student loans, and auto loans have lower rates of interest, while credit cards, "payday loans," and store cards cost you more.

According to CNBC (2020), "good" debt is defined as money owed for things that can help build wealth or increase income over time, such as student loans, mortgages, or business loans. "Bad" debt refers to things like credit cards or other consumer debt that do little to improve your financial outcome. Zone in on paying off the "bad" debts to keep them off your balance sheet. With high rates of interest, those debts will keep growing even if you're not adding to them.

As many people in Generations X, Y, and Z have discovered, while student loan debt is considered "good" debt, it can take *years* and several thousand dollars in interest to shake off the balance sheet. The folks in these cohorts who graduated from college in the years surrounding the epic market downturns of 2001 and 2008 likely accepted jobs for lower pay than they deserved, went back to school to "wait it out" and piled on more debt, or couldn't get a job at all. This limited their ability to pay down these debts in their early working years, and now they've carried it for ten to fifteen years or longer. Ideally, you borrow less than your expected first year salary. So, if a job in your field pays $55,000 in the first year, you should have less than that in student loans to acquire that degree. "This guideline is premised on the notion that with yearly salary increases, you should be able to keep up with the interest in your debt and pay it off within the standard ten-year repayment window" (CNBC 2020).

For many folks, their mortgage is their largest liability as it is matched up with their biggest asset—their home. The rule of thumb is your mortgage payment should be no more than 28 percent to 33 percent of your income. In addition, you want to keep your total debt to income ratio (your monthly debt payments including the mortgage, divided by your income) below 40 percent. Don't forget, now that you have a little one, the average cost for full-time day care at a center is $972 per month on top of your debt payments (BabyCenter.com).

Once you have more than one child in daycare, it is very likely your monthly daycare bill will be more than your mortgage.

As you pay down liabilities, your overall net worth grows. If you carry balances on credit cards, zone in on paying those off first. Credit cards charge an insane amount of interest and are working against you constantly. Those balances can cause you stress, bring your credit score down, and limit your ability to obtain other debt, like mortgages and business loans. Once your credit cards are paid off, set your sights on paying down student loans, car loans, or other debts outside of your mortgage. Mathematically, it makes sense to pay off the debts with higher interest rates first, but make sure you don't miss a payment on any of them or you may be hit with penalties and cause some damage to your credit score. The fewer liabilities you have, the more flexibility you have with where your money goes each month. More liabilities equal more payments and less *freedom*.

WHERE SHOULD YOUR NET WORTH BE?

Where should your net worth be today? My response to that question is "higher than it was at this time last year." The real benchmark that matters is that *your* net worth is growing and getting better over time. Sure, it might fluctuate and go down some years (like 2008–2009 for instance), but it should be trending upward over a timeline of three years or greater.

There are some targets you can shoot for. Like with everything in personal finance, there is not a one-size-fits-all answer, but I will provide you with some guidelines and rules of thumb.

According to Thomas Stanley and William Danko, authors of *The Millionaire Next Door*, you can calculate your ideal net worth target using the following formula:

(Age x Pre-tax Income)/10 = Your Ideal Net Worth

Take your age multiplied by your income (before taxes are taken out), then divide by ten. This is about where your net worth (all assets minus all liabilities) should be today. Remember, this is just a ballpark—especially if your income has been increasing quite a bit over the last few years. So, if you are thirty-six years old with a salary of $75,000 a year, your ideal net worth target is $270,000.

Typically for folks in the millennial/Gen X age group, the portion of your net worth that is growing the most each year is the retirement asset bucket, usually in company retirement plans—like 401(k)s—or individual accounts—like IRAs and Roth IRAs.

Here are some rules of thumb for the retirement savings bucket:

- Target 10 to 15 percent of total income to long-term savings.
- By age thirty, have *half* of your annual income in retirement savings.
- By age forty, have *twice* your annual income in retirement savings.

- By age fifty, have *four times* your annual income in retirement savings.

How do you measure up to the rules of thumb? Are you right on track, or do you have some work to do? As I discussed in chapter one, it's not about where you are right now. It's the trajectory you're on going forward that really matters. Maybe you are currently only saving 3 percent of your income toward retirement. That's okay; it's actually a great start! Where you go from here is to start creeping that percentage up when you can. Remember what James Clear, the author of *Atomic Habits*, said? If you make even a 1 percent increase each year, that will add up over time. Boost your contribution rate up 1 to 2 percent to start and see if you even notice a difference. Every year, bump it up another percentage point until you get to that 10 to 15 percent range. If you get a 3 percent merit increase, allocate 1 percent of it toward retirement before that bigger paycheck hits.

NET WORTH IN YOUR TWENTIES—STARTING TO BUILD

Generally, in your twenties is where you want to work to get that net worth into positive territory. Start paying down student loans and start building retirement accounts. These are likely low-income years for the most part. You might still be in school, in residency, or in entry-level positions. It is difficult to start building net worth, but remember, even 1 percent adds up in the end.

NET WORTH IN YOUR THIRTIES AND FORTIES—
WHERE THE MAGIC HAPPENS

The thirties and forties is where a lot of rapid growth happens. According to the Financial Samurai, you should target growing your net worth by 10 to 50 percent each year during this phase. This is when we start gaining traction in our careers and mastering our trades. Maybe we move into management roles and have higher income and bonus potential each year. We have finally paid off the student loans (or the bulk of them), own a home, and have been consistently contributing to retirement accounts for several years. You might finally feel like you're starting to get ahead. This also is generally the time of having kids, so more expenses come into play.

Remember, these are just ballpark targets and rules of thumb. Everyone's situation is unique, and we are all starting from different places and have faced our own setbacks and challenges along the way. The important thing is your net worth this year is bigger than your net worth last year.

TIME VALUE OF MONEY—THE NET
WORTH SUPER-BOOSTER

According to Investopedia, time value of money is the concept that money you have now is worth more than the identical sum in the future due to its earning capacity. So, one dollar invested today is worth more than one dollar invested in the future. This is due to compounding interest and investment returns. Essentially, you earn interest on your initial deposit, and then that interest also starts earning interest, so your savings grow much faster over time. The same principal applies to investment returns, but on a bigger scale. If you leave your money and the returns you earn invested in the market, those returns are compounded over time in the same way that interest is compounded. The sooner you start that compounding, the more magical it becomes!

Here are some examples of how powerful the compounding can be over time:
Aliyah and Paige are both contributing to their company 401(k) plan and are invested in a growth allocation of 80 percent equity and 20 percent fixed income. For the sake of this example, their money will earn 8 percent a year (in real life, this number would be higher in some years and lower in others, but it is an average). Aliyah is an early bird and started contributing to the 401(k) at the age of twenty-five. She contributed $200 a month from age twenty-five to age thirty-five, then fell off the wagon and stopped contributing altogether. With the power of compounding returns, at age sixty-five, Aliyah has a 401(k) balance of $400,138.

Paige read this book at the age of thirty-five and decided it was time to get a system in place to start contributing to her 401(k). She also started contributing $200 per month and continued that until age sixty-five. Paige's retirement account balance at age sixty-five is $298,071. She ended up with less than Aliyah at age sixty-five even though she contributed for a much longer period.

Investor	Monthly Amount Contributed	Years Contributing	Balance at age 65
Aliyah	$200	Age 25–35 (10 years)	$400,138
Paige	$200	Age 35–63 (30 years)	$298,071

The power of compounding interest and starting early

Aliyah had the power of time on her side. The more time money has to compound and grow, the more amazing the results are. The sooner you start, the better.

"The best time to plant a tree was twenty years ago. The second-best time is now."

—CHINESE PROVERB

"MONEY BOSS" SYSTEMS FOR SUCCESS SUMMARY—CHAPTER 2

- Always have an emergency fund of three to six months' worth of expenses available.
  - Pro tip: Hide the fund from yourself by putting it in an online bank account that earns interest.

- Automation is key.
  - Have a portion of your paycheck directly deposited into your emergency fund.
  - Boost your 401(k) savings rate 1 to 2 percent a year until you are contributing 10 to 15 percent annually or maxing out.

- Compounding returns are your best friend.
  - Start investing sooner rather than later.

- Don't let debt eat you alive.
  - Your mortgage payment should be no more than 28 to 33 percent of your monthly income.
  - Your overall monthly debt payments (mortgage, student loans, car loans, etc.) divided by your monthly income should be less than 40 percent.
  - Work to keep "bad" debts off your balance sheet for good.

- Net worth building rules of thumb include the following:
  - Target 10 to 15 percent of total income to long-term savings.
  - By age thirty, have *half* of your annual income in retirement savings.
  - By age forty, have *twice* your annual income in retirement savings.
  - By age fifty, have *four times* your annual income in retirement savings.

CHAPTER 3

CASH FLOW—WHERE THE MAGIC HAPPENS

———

"Become so financially secure that
you forget it's payday."

—UNKNOWN

I see you. Your hard work is finally starting to pay off. The student loan balances are gone, your career is taking off, and your income has increased every year for the last five years. I know you are busy juggling the costs and demands of parenthood and feel like you're overwhelmed and sometimes out of control. I know you dread reading this chapter because you *think* it's about the blasphemous "B" word—*budgeting* (insert spooky horror movie music). The thing is you are not alone. I have worked in the financial industry since 2004, and issues with cash flow are a common theme for everyone at all levels. It doesn't matter if you make $30,000 a year or $300,000 a year—managing cash flow is *hard*. According to Mint.com, 65 percent of Americans have no idea how much they spent last month. Nearly a third of Americans surveyed said they wish they had spent less in the last month.

This is a bigger problem than you realize. According to Nielsen data, the American Payroll Association, Career-Builder, and the National Endowment for Financial Education, somewhere between 50 to 78 percent of American workers are living paycheck to paycheck (note: some data is from 2019, during the government shutdown, and 2020, during the COVID-19 pandemic). That means more than half the population could have a disaster on their hands if they miss just one payday. They are in a constant state of worry with that sick, panicky feeling in the pits of their stomachs. According to a study by Ramsey Solutions, arguments related to spending are the second leading cause for divorce, behind infidelity. Managing cash flow is challenging, but it doesn't have to cost your sanity or wreak havoc on your marriage.

As we discussed in chapter one, we don't always handle our money with the rational side of the brain. The way we spend money is ingrained in who we are because of our upbringing, our culture, our Money Scripts®, and our habits. Overcoming those is no small feat. You can't just say, "I want to spend less money," without addressing the emotion behind it. That isn't powerful enough to make a lasting change.

You feel ashamed. You are a thirty-something successful career builder who seems to have it all together on the outside, yet you feel like there is some sort of magic potion others have that you haven't discovered yet.

What if I told you it doesn't have to be this hard? What if there was a way to align your spending with your values that didn't feel like a punishment? What if I told you things could be a lot simpler, and you could actually pay less attention to what you spend each month?

Dave Ramsey, Suzie Orman, and your grandma Flossy all say, "You need a budget!" while wagging a stern finger in your direction. They are right; budgets are a great tool. If you are good at keeping a budget, and it works for your household, then hallelujah! You spreadsheet-loving champs are the exception and not the rule. I am a big fan of yours. For the rest of us, I have a different solution involving automation and limiting the number of decisions you must make about your spending each month.

On the one hand, you have known expenses that happen every month—your mortgage, trash bill, cell phone bill, etc.—and these expenses are easy to track. Then there are always those one-offs that only happen once or twice a year that throw you for a loop. Some of these items are things we know are coming, but they surprise us anyway—Christmas, time to renew your Kansas State Wildcat season tickets, summer camps, braces, etc. Not to mention all the costly accidents, like driving your car through the garage door when it's not all the way open (purely hypothetical example here—never actually happened to me), windows or legs getting broken, the deep freezer dying when it is full of food, so you need to buy a replacement and get it up and running as soon as possible! Life happens, and cash flow needs are not always predictable.

Budget—and we are back to that infamous, dreaded "B" word! Everyone *hates* budgeting—including me. Why do we hate it so much? We hate it because it feels restrictive, like you can never buy things or have fun. Or when you are buying things, you must bargain shop and not buy what you really want. It's like dieting when all you want is a plate of sour cream-coated nachos.

What I am going to share with you is not budgeting in the traditional, blood-sucking sense. It is creating a spending plan, a way to manage cash flow so you are saving, working toward your goals, and developing a better understanding how much you can spend each month on fun stuff without damaging long-term objectives. You want to live well today while planning for the future. Getting command of cash flow means you are making sure all your fixed expenses as well as things that might come up throughout the year are taken care of, being ready for those inevitable surprises, and enjoying your money today.

A CASH FLOW MANAGEMENT SYSTEM THAT WORKS

"The expert at anything was once a beginner."
—HELEN HAYES

Here is an example of a system that works for many people who are trying to get organized. It is a "bucket" or modern day "envelope" system that I will illustrate for you. What is an "envelope" system? Here's a quick history lesson. Back in the olden days (like the 1990s), people were often paid by their employers with a physical check that they would then walk to the bank to convert to cash. Direct deposit existed back then, but not everyone was on board. Once they got their wad of cash, they would divvy it up into envelopes—one labeled "rent," one labeled "groceries," one labeled "bills," etc. This helped them make sure the bills were paid and they did not overspend in any category. If they were standing in line at the grocery checkout and the total was more than the cash in their "grocery" envelope, they would have to put some things back, and *voilà!* They stayed within the budget for groceries. These days, everything is electronic, so it is incredibly easy to overspend without even realizing where the overspending is occurring.

In my example, which is modeled after my personal system, we use five "buckets" (bank accounts), each with a different purpose. Picture five buckets lined up horizontally across the page. Using five accounts may seem more complicated, but trust me, it actually eliminates confusion and cuts down on surprise expenses. Here is a run-down of our bucket system:

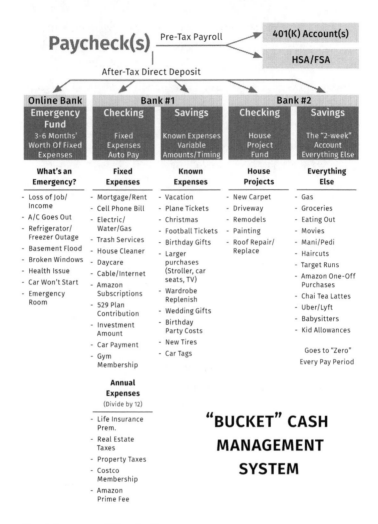

Paycheck(s) — Pre-Tax Payroll → 401(K) Account(s) / HSA/FSA

After-Tax Direct Deposit

Online Bank	Bank #1		Bank #2	
Emergency Fund	**Checking**	**Savings**	**Checking**	**Savings**
3-6 Months' Worth Of Fixed Expenses	Fixed Expenses Auto Pay	Known Expenses Variable Amounts/Timing	House Project Fund	The "2-week" Account Everything Else
What's an Emergency?	**Fixed Expenses**	**Known Expenses**	**House Projects**	**Everything Else**
- Loss of Job/ Income	- Mortgage/Rent	- Vacation	- New Carpet	- Gas
- A/C Goes Out	- Cell Phone Bill	- Plane Tickets	- Driveway	- Groceries
- Refrigerator/ Freezer Outage	- Electric/ Water/Gas	- Christmas	- Remodels	- Eating Out
- Basement Flood	- Trash Services	- Football Tickets	- Painting	- Movies
- Broken Windows	- House Cleaner	- Birthday Gifts	- Roof Repair/ Replace	- Mani/Pedi
- Health Issue	- Daycare	- Larger purchases (Stroller, car seats, TV)		- Haircuts
- Car Won't Start	- Cable/Internet	- Wardrobe Replenish		- Target Runs
- Emergency Room	- Amazon Subscriptions	- Wedding Gifts		- Amazon One-Off Purchases
	- 529 Plan Contribution	- Birthday Party Costs		- Chai Tea Lattes
	- Investment Amount	- New Tires		- Uber/Lyft
	- Car Payment	- Car Tags		- Babysitters
	- Gym Membership			- Kid Allowances
				Goes to "Zero" Every Pay Period

Annual Expenses
(Divide by 12)

- Life Insurance Prem.
- Real Estate Taxes
- Property Taxes
- Costco Membership
- Amazon Prime Fee

"BUCKET" CASH MANAGEMENT SYSTEM

Jamie's personal "bucket" system.

We each bring home a paycheck twice a month. On a pre-tax basis, our contributions to our 401(k)s (retirement accounts), flexible spending account for health care, and flexible spending account for dependent care come out automatically. So, we are paying ourselves right off the bat by having funds going into our retirement accounts before we can spend them. On an after-tax basis, the remaining dollars are split up as follows:

BUCKET #1—ONLINE BANK

This is our emergency fund. We use an online bank to keep these funds "out of sight, out of mind" by not keeping them in the accounts we use for regular monthly expenses. We also benefit by using an online bank because they are paying a higher interest rate than most brick-and-mortar banks are offering as I write this. If you are leaving money in cash, it might as well be earning something. This account is linked to our regular checking accounts so we can transfer funds as needed. We have a direct deposit from our paychecks set up until we get to a balance we are comfortable with. The target is to have three to six months' worth of fixed expenses in this account that are available and liquid in the event of an emergency. What counts as an emergency? A loss of income, hospitalization, issues with the home that need to be fixed quickly (think flooding, broken windows, freezer breaks, etc.) count, not *Christmas* or *summer camp*! We basically try to ignore this account and let it grow so it will be there when we need it.

The remaining buckets are lifestyle and short-term goal buckets. I split them up between two different banks, so I only have one checking account and one savings account per institution. This makes it easier on me to remember because the debit cards do not look the same.

BUCKET #2—CHECKING ACCOUNT 1: LIFESTYLE FIXED

This bucket is for our fixed expenses that happen regularly. They are known amounts, and we set them all up on auto-pay if possible. These are expenses like the mortgage, cell phone bills, trash service, daycare tuition, cable, and even regular expenses, like our Amazon Prime Subscribe & Save items that are the same each month. This account also funds expenses that happen once a year in known amounts, like life insurance premiums and our Costco and Amazon Prime membership fees. We simply map out how much these cost each year and divide by twelve. We have that amount deposited each month into this account so the annual amount will be available when the bill is due.

We also use this account to automate some savings goals and charitable donations. We have prioritized building 529 education plan funds for the kids as well as building an investment balance outside of company retirement plans. So, we've essentially made the savings for those goals a "bill" that is paid automatically each month to make sure we are forcing ourselves to contribute to those goals. This is another way to "pay yourself first." You force the savings and make it automatic so you don't just spend those dollars as you might if they were just sitting in your bank account. It is the same with charitable donations. We have an automatic draft set up to our church and account for it as if it is a bill that must be paid.

BUCKET #3—SAVINGS ACCOUNT 1: LIFESTYLE AND SHORT-TERM GOALS

This is for known expenses that vary in amount and timing, but you know they will likely happen. For instance, vacation and travel, season tickets to sporting events, Christmas gifts, and larger purchases, like furniture or electronics. We simply estimate how much we will need for the year for these items and divide by twelve to determine how much we want to put into this bucket each month. When we need the funds to book a trip or make a purchase, we simply transfer the funds to the checking account (Bucket 2 above) and pay for it.

BUCKET #4—SAVINGS ACCOUNT 2: SHORT-TERM, SPECIFIC GOALS

For us, this bucket is our house project fund. We have identified several things we would like to do to our home and know there will be other items to update eventually, like replacing the roof or water heater. We build this bucket up with monthly deposits, and when it reaches a certain amount, we decide if we want to start on a project. When we are ready to use it, we simply transfer the funds to the checking account at Bank #2 (below) and pay for it. Both of these savings buckets tend to have rolling balances. For instance, when we had the exterior of our house painted, that took a large chunk of what was in the house project fund bucket. After that, we need to let the funds build back up before choosing to do the next project.

Here's a pro tip: you should always plan on spending money for home upkeep each year. The rule of thumb is you should set aside at least 1 percent of your home's value every year for maintenance. For a $300,000 home, this works out to be $3,000 a year or $250 a month. If you are a homeowner, you know there are always things that need to be fixed or updated, or things that go wrong. The water heater needs to be replaced, the walls need painting, the kids use the toy drill to poke a hole in the playroom drywall, a family of bats move into your attic—the joys of home ownership.

BUCKET #5—CHECKING ACCOUNT 2: LIFESTYLE DISCRETIONARY

This is the "two-week" account that is a catch-all for basically everything else. These are our normal weekly expenditures for gas, groceries, eating out, haircuts, coffee runs, Uber rides, etc. Since all our other goals are being funded and bills are paid, this account can basically go to zero dollars each pay cycle. This is the account we use most often in the form of a debit card. It also forces some communication between me and my husband about the expenses we expect for the next two weeks. If we know we are going on a Costco run that will cost a few hundred dollars, we know to spend less in other areas and may skip eating out or getting a manicure during that time frame.

If you find there is too much in this bucket, you can pump up your savings and increase 401(k) contributions if you are not already maxing out. Alternatively, you could start directing some excess monthly dollars to a Roth IRA, to another investment account, to other goals, or to expedite home projects. If you find that there is not any money left after figuring out your fixed and regular living expenses, you may be overextended. You will need to go back through your expenses to see if there are any subscriptions that could be cut or ways to reduce spending on things that aren't a priority for you. If there is a large disparity, you may have to adjust your lifestyle (or increase your income) significantly by downsizing your house, your rent, or your car.

GETTING THE BUCKETS TO WORK FOR YOU

You may need more or fewer buckets depending on the expenses you have and what you want to fund, but having dollars earmarked for specific goals and expenses has really helped my family and countless clients manage monthly finances. It does take a while to adjust to a new system like this, so be patient with yourself, and give yourself time to adapt. A good time to start the system is when you have extra cash from bonus time or a tax refund to get the buckets started before your direct deposits are set up. I would recommend keeping a chart of your buckets so you remember which expenses should come from each account. Once the system is up and running, you have fewer decisions to make. Your savings and bill pay are all automated, so you are really just dealing with the cash in the "two-week" bucket each pay period. You don't have to worry if you can spend your money on happy hour or if it needs to go to the cell phone bill because that bill has already been accounted for.

The biggest upfront task is mapping out how much should go to each bucket. I think the easiest place to start is with the two checking account buckets. First, figure out the fixed expense bucket. Those are usually easy to find in your bank account transactions, but don't forget about the annual expenses, like life insurance premiums, which are larger chunks. Then you can ballpark the "two-week" account expenses by targeting an amount for gas, groceries, and normal incidentals. You could look back at your bank account history or use a service like Mint.com to figure out what you might want to target here. Once you know how much you need for all the fixed and living expenses, you can figure out how much to allocate to the savings buckets. If you do not have a fully funded emergency fund now, I would suggest prioritizing this until you get to a balance of at least $5,000 before building up a house project or vacation fund. Maybe you only need three accounts—maybe you need six, but the important thing is everyone who has a debit card in your household knows what it can be used for.

Some couples want to maintain individual checking accounts instead of jointly owning all of them. I am completely fine with that. Just make sure you are both on the same page as to what the priorities are and how much goes into each account for the month.

Once you figure out how much needs to go into each account each month, the key is to get the direct deposit set up so you don't have to think about it each payday. If you must manually transfer funds to different bank accounts, you are much less likely to do it. James Clear, the author of *Atomic Habits,* says one of the big keys to establishing a good habit is to *make it easy.* As humans, we tend to default to the path of least resistance, so purposely make saving and paying bills an easy habit for you. Don't just say, "I want to save more." Set up your financial systems so it happens automatically before you have the chance to do something different with the money. It is easier not to spend money if it's never in your hands to begin with.

"But what about my credit card points?" Many people like to use credit cards to earn points or travel rewards on their daily purchases. I'm cool with that as long as you pay the balances off each month. An easy way to incorporate credit cards into this bucket system is to use a credit card for the "two week" bucket. You've made a plan for how much you can spend each pay period from that bucket, so you just have to keep your charges below that amount each month.

If you are struggling with monthly spending, give this "bucket" approach a try! Managing cash flow can be tricky, but if you plan for what is coming and have command of your spending, you will set yourself up for success.

ALIGNING YOUR MONEY WITH YOUR VALUES

"Too many people spend money they earned to buy things they don't want to impress people that they don't like."

—WILL ROGERS

Hannah Moore, owner of Guiding Wealth and the creator of the Everyday Money Budgeting Blocks System, has some really cool insights on aligning your money with what you value. In our interview, she said, "Every budget should tell a story, and yours should look different than everyone else's."

It should look different from your brother's, your sister's, and your neighbor's because we don't all fit into the same mold. Budgeting has such a negative connotation because we always start the conversation with "Where can we make cuts?" Instead, Hannah says we should start with "Where do we love to spend money?" Before talking numbers, she has each client complete a values exercise. This helps them envision what their life would look like if their money was aligned with those values.

There is so much shame around spending and so many "shoulds." We think we "should" be doing this or "should" be doing that. We must stop "shoulding" ourselves and think about what we really want out of life. A lot of people say things like, "We should stop eating out so much." Well, how does that align with your values? If you enjoy going out to eat and treasure that experience with your family, then it could be argued eating out is a priority. On the flip side, if you value vacations and haven't been able to take trips because all your funds are spent each month, you may ask yourself, "What do I value more?" If the family time on vacation is more important than eating out, you might choose to eat out less to allocate more to the vacation fund. When we flip the script, you are now making a conscious choice to put your money where your values are, so it doesn't feel like a chore or feel like you're depriving yourself of something.

Hannah's Everyday Money Budgeting Blocks system is really cool because it makes your money more tangible. You can buy her kit online and will receive a workbook and a set of three hundred actual building blocks to bring your spending to life. Once you have the blocks laid out in a way that represents your spending now, you can then rearrange them to illustrate how you'd *like* to be spending your money.

"Don't tell me where your priorities are. Show me where you spend your money, and I'll tell you what they are."

—JAMES W. FRICK

The cash flow conversation is so important. Financial planning overall is about building a framework for organizing all the pieces of your financial life so you can make better decisions and you can see how those decisions impact all the other areas of your life. How you use your money impacts every area of your financial plan. It's about cash flow, investing, and saving, which impacts not only how you live today but also what your future looks like. Other areas it touches are how prepared you are for risks—insurance-related topics and estate planning. Not to mention taxes and all the short and long-term goals you want to achieve. So, if we think of all these topics as bricks in the framework we are building, then cash flow is the cement that holds the bricks together and makes the framework strong. It is really the linchpin in every financial plan.

If you can get command of your cash flow and start aligning your spending with the goals you want to reach, you will make progress toward those goals and objectives. Life will feel less overwhelming and more intentional. You will stop living paycheck to paycheck and move to a proactive, instead of reactive, cycle. On the flip side, if managing cash flow continues to be an issue, you will always be stressed, stretched, and uncomfortable. Surprise bills may cause you to rack up debt or take away from funds you wanted to save or invest, wrecking or delaying your plans and causing the framework to collapse.

"MONEY BOSS" SYSTEMS FOR SUCCESS—CHAPTER 3

- Limit the number of decisions you must make.
- Make it automatic.
- Make it easy.
- Align your money with your values.

CHAPTER 4

INSURING YOUR BIGGEST ASSET— YOURSELF!

"The bottom line is living isn't cheap and dying isn't free! You need a plan for both."

—DAWN CROUCH, LUTCF®, CLTC®, INSURANCE
AGENT WITH OLIVER INSURANCE AGENCY

MAKING THE CASE FOR LIFE INSURANCE— *SAVED BY THE BELL* STYLE

High school sweethearts Zack Morris and Kelly Kapowski shared a passion for teaching, and both graduated from Pepperdine as education majors. They married right out of *The College Years* and rented a tiny one-bedroom apartment in their old stomping grounds. Zack adored his high school principal, Mr. Belding, and followed in his footsteps to pursue a career in academia. He currently enjoys being a high school technology teacher and is considering getting a master's degree. Zack especially loves bringing his old Motorola DynaTAC to school to show the students what a cell phone looked like in 1991. Kelly had difficulty finding a teaching job in the area, so she did a brief stint as the Bayside High cheerleading coach. After a few years of soul-searching, Kelly decided to pursue her passion and go to law school. Somewhere along the way, they saved up enough for a down payment on a small two-bedroom house in a hip, lively neighborhood.

Fast-forward twelve years. Both Zack and Kelly are feeling fulfilled in their careers and are ready to start a family. Zack has a secure position with tenure at the high school, and Kelly has become one of California's top personal injury attorneys. The couple is now doing well financially, and once Kelly gets pregnant, they decide to upgrade to a five-bedroom house in a good school district. They welcome their first son, Mac, and find out when he is only ten months old that they are expecting twins! Daycare for two infants and a toddler is outrageous, costing more than Zack makes in salary for the year. Zack makes the tough decision to put his career on hold and stay at home with the children. The #MeToo movement has catapulted Kelly's success, and along with handling court cases, she is now asked to speak at conferences, corporate trainings, and events. This is great for their income but makes daily life tricky to navigate with Kelly's demanding work and travel schedule.

This chapter is about life insurance, so you know I am going to have to kill off these characters *Game of Thrones*-style to make my point. I will illustrate what could happen if either parent were to pass away unexpectedly.

SCENARIO #1—ZACK IS TRAGICALLY ELECTROCUTED WHILE MESSING AROUND WITH HIS BRICK MOTOROLA PHONE.

They had no life insurance on him. He had some coverage through the school when he was working but does not anymore since he left his job. Kelly earns enough money to support the family, but now she has some decisions to make that will result in some significant expenses. She will need to pay for daycare or a nanny for the three boys and will have to coordinate overnight care if she wants to keep up her travel schedule. Kelly will also likely outsource some of the other things Zack took care of throughout the day, like meal prep, cleaning, and laundry service. This adds over $5,000 a month to her existing expenses. She can either take on more work to make more money and pay for more outsourcing or cut back on her hours, making less money but saving more on the household employees.

SCENARIO #2—KELLY FALLS OFF THE STAGE DURING HER TED TALK AND IS IMPALED BY HER FOUR-INCH STILETTO HEEL.

Kelly did have some life insurance, but Zack only has one year's worth of salary through her law firm. Zack will likely be okay financially for a year, but then he will have to figure out how to earn enough to support the family *and* pay for daycare so he can work. He could pay off the house, but then he would still have to come up with enough for the real estate taxes, insurance, and maintenance, which adds up to about $20,000 a year. He could sell the house and downsize to something more affordable, but then the kids would be in a different school district. He could sell the house and move in with his pals, Lisa and Screech, or maybe his parents for a few years. He loves teaching, but he may have to get a better paying vocation or invest in more schooling or training for a different career.

According to the National Academy of Sciences, the average life expectancy in 2018 was eighty-one for females and seventy-six for males. As I write this, COVID-19 is causing a staggering death toll that may impact future life expectancy calculations. We all hope we live long, healthy lives and die of old age in our sleep, but we do not get to choose our fate. We could lose a battle with cancer, have a fatal reaction to a bee sting, get in a serious car accident, or become a victim of the coronavirus de jour. Homicide and suicide rates are growing and impact young adults every day. Zack and Kelly's tragic scenarios were just hypothetical examples of how an untimely death can devastate young parents. Death is always heart-breaking, but if you don't prepare for it, your loved ones will suffer more than they need to. If Zack had the appropriate life insurance in place, Kelly would have funds available for childcare and could continue her career and lifestyle as desired. If Kelly had the right amount of coverage in place, Zack could continue staying home with the kids and not worry about how he was going to earn income or pay the mortgage.

WHY DO I NEED IT?

If you think about it, we insure a lot of things in our lives without giving it a second thought—our homes, cars, jewelry, and bicycles. When it comes to insuring our biggest asset, *ourselves* and our ability to generate income, we tend to fall short or ignore the conversation altogether.

There are several reasons to own life insurance—business continuity planning, leaving a legacy for those you leave behind, and estate tax planning (more on this in chapter five) to name a few. The main reason for obtaining life insurance coverage as a parent is for **income replacement**. If a family income earner passes away, that income stream stops. This can be devastating to the survivors as they still must pay the mortgage, bills, food, and other necessities, not to mention paying for a funeral and saving for long-term goals, like their retirement or sending kids to college. All of this is happening while they are in an extreme state of grief, trying to mourn the death of the one they lost. Life insurance is a tool to replace that income stream and help the survivors continue their lifestyle without financial distress. You don't want those you leave behind to have to make drastic changes, like selling the home they live in or having to go back to work when they were staying home with the children.

When I say, "income replacement," that makes it clear a family income earner needs some life insurance coverage, but what about a stay-at-home parent? It is a common misconception that a person working *inside* of the home does not need life insurance coverage. Just because they are not getting paid for the work they do does not mean that work does not have financial value. According to 2019 data from Salary.com, if you are a stay-at-home mom or dad and were paid for your services, you would demand a salary of $178,201 for your around-the-clock work. (Investopedia 2020).

There are several financial factors to consider if the non-income producing spouse passes away. The working spouse will now need to find childcare and potentially find transportation to take the children to and from school or daycare. If the working spouse frequently travels, they will need to provide overnight care for the kids. The surviving spouse may need help with home maintenance, cleaning, and meal preparation if they work crazy or long hours. Losing a stay-at-home spouse can greatly affect cash flow going forward and change the lifestyle of the existing family members if they are not appropriately insured. Be sure they have at least $250,000 to $400,000 in term coverage on the non-working spouse until the kids are adults. If you have high debt balances or live in a place with a high cost of living, the amount may be higher.

Travis Tannahill with Tannahill Insurance says the biggest issue he sees is couples don't think about insuring both spouses: "They tend to only insure the higher-earning spouse (if they have insurance at all) and forget about the secondary earner or stay-at-home spouse." This is consistent with what I see as a financial planner meeting with new clients. In most cases, at least one spouse is severely underinsured.

"More than one in three parents have no life insurance at all, and the third that do have no more than $100,000 in coverage" (Bankrate.com). The average middle-class family of four in Kansas has a household income between $47,229 and $141,374 a year (Cortland 2020). If one income earner dies with $100,000 in life insurance, the family would be okay for maybe six months to a year before they had to make some really tough decisions. In an even scarier statistic, 50 percent of single parents don't have any life insurance at all (Parentology 2019).

TYPES OF LIFE INSURANCE

There are two basic types of life insurance: term and permanent. Term coverage is generally the less expensive option and is in place for a specific timeframe—usually ten, twenty, or thirty years. Permanent coverage, as the name implies, will be in place until you pass away as long as the premiums are paid and the policy is performing as expected. Permanent coverage options can take many forms including whole life, universal life, variable life, variable universal life, and even policies that include a long-term care coverage rider. Many permanent policies offer investment and savings vehicles within the policy.

WHAT TYPE DO I NEED?

Term insurance is frequently used to cover income replacement needs because the term is identifiable, and the cost is generally reasonable. For instance, you could structure the term around when your kids graduate from high school or college or around your expected retirement age. For most of us Gen X, Y, and Z parents, a twenty-year term policy will cover the bulk of the risk. Depending on your age and where you are at in your parenting cycle, a ten-year or thirty-year term may be more appropriate. There are cases where a permanent policy makes sense, like if you have a child with a disability who will be a lifelong dependent, or if you are trying to equalize an inheritance if one child is set to inherit your farm, and the life insurance could compensate the other children.

Generally speaking, term insurance is the best bang for your buck and is a great source of pure income replacement protection.

HOW MUCH DO I NEED?

A good rule of thumb to arrive at the amount of life insurance you need is seven to ten times your income. This may sound like a huge number, but replacing one's income for an extended amount of time can really add up. For instance, if the sole breadwinner of the household passes away, the surviving family members will need to replace their income to continue living life the way they have been. Besides income replacement, there are several things you should consider when evaluating your life insurance coverage, including the amount of debt you carry, your long-term plans, current and future education costs, childcare expenses, and your spending goals. If the breadwinner passes away, would the other spouse join the work force or want to continue working inside the home? Would you want the mortgage and other debts paid off so the surviving spouse does not have to worry about the payments? Would you like to have enough money to provide for your children's college education? What about your final expenses, like the funeral and burial costs?

It is a good idea to meet with a financial planner to determine what amount of life insurance and type of coverage is right for you and your loved ones. As life happens and your situation changes, you may need to adjust your life insurance coverage accordingly. Some events that could trigger a need for life insurance coverage or a change in coverage include getting married, growing your family through birth or adoption, divorce, job change, or a change to your overall health situation. Once your coverage is in place, make sure you review it every few years (or upon a triggering event) to make sure you are adequately covered.

HOW DO I GET COVERAGE?

Many employers offer life insurance for their employees, often at no cost to the employee—which is a great perk. However, it is almost never enough. Most companies offer the equivalent of one to two times your annual salary in coverage with the option to purchase more. Plus, most people do not stay with the same company for their entire working career, which could lead to a gap in coverage. I encourage folks to obtain life insurance coverage outside of their employers that way it stays in place if they have a lull in employment or move to a different company.

Insurance agent Dawn Crouch says, "When it comes to benefits through work, you can count on two things: one, if it's free, it ain't much! Two, if you're paying for coverage, you *might* be overpaying!"

It is also important to shop around. If you have an insurance agent you work with, obtain some quotes from them, but do some research to be sure you are getting a good deal. If the agent is a "captive" agent (meaning they can only write policies for a single company), you may be paying more than you should. An independent insurance broker is not "captive" and should be able to shop several companies to find you the best deal. If you are buying term insurance, the premiums are usually very reasonable and more affordable than you might think. You can check out the website Term4Sale.com to get a ballpark range of what a policy might cost you.

Do not rely on your employer to provide your life insurance—unless you have no choice. My friend Tony has had multiple kidney replacements before the age of forty. Insurance companies tend to rate people like him poorly as he is higher risk than other men his age. Workplace plans cannot deny coverage based on health history, so that may be how he gets his coverage for the time being. I have seen another interesting situation where a client was an avid sky diver and loved bungee jumping, paragliding, and other high-risk activities. Insurance companies don't like that either. He had to get his life insurance through a company-based plan as well. Pieces of your health history can play a part in whether you are able to get coverage and how you are rated (bad rating = higher cost). If you have suffered from severe depression, endured childhood cancer, or have chronic health issues, you may be best served to participate in group policies.

DO I REALLY HAVE TO PEE IN A CUP?
WHAT IS THE PROCESS LIKE?

Agent Tannahill also cited that people tend to be intimidated by the process of obtaining life insurance coverage. Let me break it down for you. There is usually a phone call or questionnaire to fill out up front about your health history. Then, they schedule a nurse to come to your house, collect some urine, blood, and stats, like your weight and blood pressure. After that, you're just waiting for the quotes to come back. The agent will contact you with the companies that offered the best rates and help you get signed up. You can pay the premium annually (they usually offer a discount if you do), quarterly, or monthly. The policy is then in place until the term expires, you stop paying premiums, or—of course—you pass away.

LIFE INSURANCE FOR PARENTS—JUST DO IT

Life insurance is a key component for protecting your family from the unknown. Hopefully, you will outlive the need for life insurance coverage, but if you don't, your family will be grateful you had it in place. Picturing your family without you in it is not fun to think or talk about, but planning ahead could make a big difference for your family's future.

LONG-TERM DISABILITY INSURANCE NEEDS

*"More people are concerned with disaster they would leave behind if they died, than the disaster they would have to **live through** if they were disabled."*

—DAWN CROUCH, LUTCF®, CLTC®, INSURANCE
AGENT WITH OLIVER INSURANCE AGENCY

Disability insurance is another area of financial planning that is typically overlooked and ignored. Disability coverage is an important consideration for parents, especially those in professions that require specific motor skills, like nurses, dentists, chiropractors, and physicians, or intense manual labor, like construction. If you can no longer do the job you trained for, how will you make money going forward? Particularly in the case of households with one income earner, an illness or injury could have devastating effects on the family lifestyle if they are not properly insured.

A WHAT-IF SCENARIO FOR DR. STRANGE

Before Dr. Stephen Strange was saving the world from dark dimension bad guys like Thanos, Kaecilius, and Dormammu, he was your standard world-renowned neurosurgeon/genius/playboy. He loved his work and was great at it. He made a lot of money and seemed to spend a lot too. He has an affinity for fancy watches and appears to live in an upscale bachelor pad with a killer view. A bad crash in the Lambo leaves his hands injured beyond repair, and he can no longer continue his career as a surgeon. As far as Dr. Strange is concerned, his life is over. The broken man travels afar on a quest to find healing where he ends up in a mirror dimension with the Ancient One, awakens his inner wizardry, and becomes the Sorcerer Supreme of the Marvel Multiverse.

What if Dr. Strange had a long-term disability policy in place before his accident? He would have still suffered the great anguish of no longer being a surgeon, but the financial piece would feel a lot better. Let's say he had an own-occupation (definitions coming soon—I promise) long-term disability policy with a one hundred and eighty-day waiting period that paid benefits to age sixty-five. This policy would replace 60 percent of his pre-disability income. He might have to downsize from the swanky condo, but having 60 percent of his prior income is better than zero. Depending on the policy, he could potentially pursue other career options while still getting his 60 percent disability payout. Maybe he finds joy in giving back to his profession as an instructor at the University of Kansas Medical Center. Then he would be collecting his teacher's salary on top of the disability pay and feel fulfilled career-wise. Maybe he starts a profitable podcast for surgeons, becomes a levitating yoga instructor, or writes books or papers for industry publications.

DISABILITY—WHAT IS THE RISK?

Disabilities are more common than you might think, and they are on the rise. According to the Social Security Administration, just over one in four of today's twenty-year-olds will become disabled before they retire. In 2020, over sixty-one million American adults were living with a disability (about 26 percent of the adult population). More than 50 percent of those disabled Americans were in their working years (defined as ages eighteen to sixty-four). Becoming disabled can put a significant strain on the family income. If the breadwinner in your household was unable to work, how would you pay your bills?

DOESN'T MY EMPLOYER COVER DISABILITY INSURANCE?

Many employers do offer disability insurance to their employees, but this type of coverage is not required. Make sure you know how much is offered through your employer and if you can purchase additional coverage if needed. You can also purchase coverage outside of your employer through an insurance broker. Work with your financial planner to determine if the amount you are covered for currently would be enough to support your family's bills and ongoing needs. If not, you should investigate getting more coverage.

WHAT ELSE SHOULD I CONSIDER?

Even if you do have coverage, most disability policies have a waiting period of thirty, sixty, ninety, or one hundred and eighty days before benefits pay out. Do you have enough in cash reserves or your emergency fund to meet your obligations during this time frame? If your employer currently pays the premiums for your disability coverage, any benefits you receive will be taxable to you upon receipt; make sure you consider this in your calculations. Also consider a disability's impact on your long-term plans. Factor in amounts you are saving in your company 401(k) and other savings amounts required to meet your retirement goals.

You'll want to understand if your policy is an "own-occupation" or "any-occupation" policy. Generally speaking, an own-occupation policy would pay out if you had a condition that prevented you from doing the basic duties of your current occupation. An any-occupation policy would kick in only if you were unable to work in any vocation.

KEY CHAPTER TAKEAWAY:

Once you have people that depend on you for financial support, insurance becomes a critical factor in your overall financial plan. Do not forget to insure your most important asset (your ability to make income) by making sure life insurance and disability coverage are a part of your overall risk management program.

"MONEY BOSS" SYSTEMS FOR SUCCESS SUMMARY—CHAPTER 4

- If someone depends on your income to fund their lifestyle, you need life insurance coverage.
- Term coverage is the best bang for your buck. A twenty- to thirty-year term policy should cover the bulk of the risk for a Gen X, Y, or Z parent.
- Here's the rule of thumb: you need seven to ten times your income in life insurance coverage (pro tip—hire a

financial planner to calculate the right amount of coverage for your family).

- The stay-at-home spouse needs life insurance coverage too (likely at least $250,000 to $400,000).
- Disabilities are more prevalent than you think and could damage your ability to earn income. Understand the coverage you have through work and potentially look to add more coverage.

CHAPTER 5

ESTATE PLANNING— WHAT EVERY PARENT NEEDS TO KNOW

"In this world, nothing can be said to be certain, except death and taxes."

—BENJAMIN FRANKLIN

ROMEO AND JULIET—THE REMIX

"O Romeo, Romeo, wherefore art thou Romeo?"

Everyone knows the classic tale of the star-crossed lovers who took their lives because of a family vendetta that forbade them from being together. What if things were different? What if the message about the fake poison had reached Romeo in time? For the sake of a lesson in estate planning, here is an equally tragic alternative ending for this unlucky young couple.

After finding out Juliet faked her death because of a silly family feud, the Montagues and Capulets had an awakening, went to some group therapy, and are working out their differences. Romeo and Juliet are allowed to wed, and everything is looking up. Cue the cupcakes and rainbows.

However, the wedding is a total train wreck—some sword fights break out, Uncle Barnabas is passed out under the cake table, and Mercutio makes some colorful comments about Juliet's mom in his best man speech. Turns out, the families are still in archnemesis status but are attempting to tolerate each other for the kids' sake.

To escape all the drama, the newlyweds plan to keep their distance for a while. Juliet hyphenates her name to keep her parents happy, and they move into a little farmhouse a couple of kingdoms down. Juliet gets pregnant on their honeymoon in Florence just a few weeks later. The duo wants to try to make it on their own and start their own family tree, so Romeo gets a job as a medical sales representative for the local apothecary.

Business is good in medicine, but word on the street is flavors and fragrance are where the real money is. Romeo starts to branch out and creates a new line of perfumes, extracts, and food flavorings. The folks in Verona go wild for the flavors he has created; they really spice up the weekly provisions. Romeo is on the hunt for more office space, but for now, all the flavors are stored right next to the medicines, poisons, and potions.

Juliet gives birth to triplets that next spring. Reginald, Wolfgang, and Clementine Capulet-Montague are added to the story line. Now that they have dependents, Romeo and Juliet know they should get wills drafted. They are busy, tired, and overwhelmed, so they keep putting off the meeting with the village estate planning attorney.

In their exhausted state, they hadn't quite figured out the labeling system for the elixirs, and in true Shakespearean fashion, Romeo grabs a vial of nightshade instead of vanilla bean flavoring. After a sleepless night, he makes steamy mugs of vanilla chai tea lattes for himself and his lovely bride to start the day. Pour one out for our homies, the lovebirds.

Romeo and Juliet died without a will, so no one knew who they would have selected to be guardians of the kids. Would they have chosen one of their parents? A sibling, perhaps? Would they have chosen Juliet's second cousin, Tybalt, or her ex-fiancé, Paris? Maybe Romeo's trusted servant, Balthasar? Lord and Lady Montague assumed they would be the obvious choice for guardianship of the triplets. Naturally, the Capulets wanted the children to join their house. This incites a seventeen-year court battle, and the triplets live in foster care with Friar Laurence until the case can be resolved. Young Reg, Wolfy, and Clem turn eighteen and move to Milan to start a new life, free of their grandparents' drama. The Capulet and Montague rivalry rages on, and the families hate each other until the end of time.

Final curtain

BASIC PARTS OF AN ESTATE PLAN

No one likes to think about their own demise, but let's face it, there is a 100 percent chance we are going to die at some point. We all plan for long and healthy lives, but we do not get to choose how much sand is in our proverbial hourglass. If death is certain, then why do so many people choose to die without a plan? According to the 2020 estate planning study by Caring.com, less than one-third (32 percent) of Americans have a will in place. In my experience, people either do not want to think about the prospect of dying, or they have no idea where to start, so they procrastinate or do nothing.

Everything you own is your "estate." When you die, there are legal processes in place to transfer the assets in your estate appropriately. Making an estate plan puts you in the driver's seat of directing where those assets go instead of letting the court or the state decide.

People often get paralysis by analysis when there is a lot to think about, and they get overwhelmed and tend to shut down. I am going to list out the things you need to think about for each estate planning document and how to get them in place, so you are ready to act. Five basic parts of an estate plan are outlined below. We'll start with definitions, and then I'll explain a little more about why it's important to you as a parent. Note—these documents need to be drafted by an attorney or a legal service provider. I'll show you how to find one later in this chapter.

LAST WILL AND TESTAMENT

This document deals with the distribution of your assets/ property at death, names an executor (person in charge of carrying out the will), and if applicable, names guardians for your children/pets.

- Each person in a couple needs a will.
- **Guardian(s)**—This is the biggest line item to discuss. Who would you want to raise your kids if you were no longer around? It is best to come up with at least a couple of options here. Name your first choice, then have some backups listed in case the first choice isn't available. You can name anyone you want—friends, cousins, siblings, parents, etc. You can choose who your children would live with and also who would be in charge of any financial assets you leave to them (doesn't have to be the same person). Maybe your little sister Sarah is your first choice of who the kids would live with if you're not around. However, Sarah tends to be a big spender and isn't super responsible with money. In that case, you could nominate your cousin Ralph, the accountant, to oversee the financial side.
- **Executor(s)**—This is the person who oversees making sure the desires in your will are carried out. Usually, spouses or partners select each other first, then another party as a successor (i.e., a replacement in case the first person you list is unable to serve). You can choose a person (or people) or an institution, like a bank or trust company, to serve. As with the guardians, you will want to list out a few options in order of preference.

- What happens to the tangible property (cars, clothing, household items, etc.)? Usually, everything you own is transferred to your spouse, partner, or kids. If there is a specific jewelry item or keepsake you want to go to someone in particular, this is where you lay that out.
- What happens to the intangible property (investments without a named beneficiary)?
    - When the first person in a marriage/partnership passes, the intangible property is typically transferred to the other.
    - If your partner is no longer around, you might designate the assets to go to your kids. You'll need to decide if the kids will receive the money outright or if a trust should be created to manage it for them. You can put some age restrictions on it. For instance, many people choose to have the funds available for health, education, maintenance, and support immediately, but allow the trustee (person you leave in charge) to govern whether the expense is approved. In addition, you might set up a timeline for the kids to receive the remainder of the funds outright.
        - A common setup is to have them receive a third of their share at age twenty-five, a third at age thirty, and the rest at age thirty-five. You get to choose the age brackets you feel are appropriate. Breaking up the distributions gives the kids a chance to make mistakes. If they get their first distribution at age twenty-five and blow it in three months, hopefully they've learned a lesson and will be more careful at the next distribution point.

- This is ancillary, but if your heirs do not survive, who would you want to get your assets? You might name a charity, your alma mater, siblings, extended family, etc.

TRUST

A trust is a legal entity created by a party (the grantor—you) through which a second party (the trustee—whoever you leave in charge when you're gone) holds the right to manage assets and property for the benefit of a third party (the beneficiary—likely your children/heirs).

- Not everyone needs a trust, but everyone does need a will (more on this to come).
- A trust becomes active the day you create it, unlike a will, which becomes active after one's death.
- Trusts offer more control of assets but are more tedious to set up, more expensive, and require more ongoing management.

HEALTHCARE POWER OF ATTORNEY

In this document, you nominate who can talk with the doctors on your behalf in the event you are incapacitated.

- This is the person who can make decisions on your behalf concerning your medical condition, treatment, and care (so make sure they like you!).
- First powerholder (typically spouse/partner).
- Successor powerholders (two backups are recommended).

LIVING WILL/ADVANCED MEDICAL DIRECTIVE

This is the "when to pull the plug" document. You can specify any religious wishes/beliefs for the doctors to follow and decide when you no longer want life-sustaining measures taken if your demise is imminent.

- This document lets your health care team and loved ones know what kind of care you want to receive if you are not able to communicate it.

DURABLE POWER OF ATTORNEY (FINANCIAL)

A durable power of attorney allows you to authorize someone to act on your behalf to do things like pay your bills, file your taxes, and supervise your investments if you are unable to do so. You can make this authorization effective immediately or effective upon a certain event.

- This is the person who takes care of your financial affairs in the event you are still alive but incapacitated.
- You will need to choose the first powerholder (typically spouse/partner).
- Then choose a couple of successor powerholders (two backups are recommended).

It is generally a good idea to notify the people you have nominated to serve in these roles so they aren't taken by surprise and can ask you questions about your preferences *before* something happens to you.

All these documents can be changed or altered while you are alive and have mental capacity. So, if you want to change your guardians or who's in charge of your health care, you can do that at any time. A change to a will is called a **"codicil"** and can be done by an attorney.

WHY THIS MATTERS TO YOU

It is common to think wills and other estate planning documents only apply to "wealthy people" who have a lot of money and other items that need to be passed on to specific individuals or family members. Sure, having an estate plan is imperative for wealthy folks, like Oprah, Beyonce, and Jeff Bezos, but if you are a parent, it should matter to you as well.

Creating a will is one of the most important things you can do to make sure your child is cared for by the people you would choose if anything should happen to you. Your will is where you designate a guardian to care for your child or children if you die before they become adults. You can also designate a property guardian (usually referred to as a trustee) to manage your money for your children until they are old enough to manage it on their own. These roles can be filled by the same person, or you can choose two different people to carry out the separate roles.

You guys, I know this is no fun to think about, but it's super important. If you don't make these decisions, some stranger in a courtroom will decide for you. You don't want your kids to be stuck in foster care, like the Capulet-Montague triplets, while their fate is decided in a court battle.

WILLS VS. TRUSTS

My biggest concern for parents in the estate planning space is making sure the kids are provided for and getting guardians listed in their wills. I mentioned creating a trust under your will for minor children that would go into effect at your death if the kids were still minors. There is also the option of creating a "revocable living trust" you can change while you are alive but becomes irrevocable (unable to be changed) at your death. Creating a trust in your plan now offers a higher level of protection and privacy but is more expensive to set up and more tedious to maintain. If you have a trust, you will still need a will that directs assets into the trust (called a pour-over will). If you create a living trust now, you should retitle your assets into the name of the trust. For example, your home should be retitled into the name of the trust as well as investment accounts, beneficiary designations, and other items you own.

When you die, there is a legal process that takes place called "probate." If you have a will, the probate process will involve proving your will is valid, executing your instructions, and paying any applicable taxes. If you do not have a will, this process is drawn out longer as the court figures out how to transfer your assets via state requirements. If you own property in multiple states, your estate will be subject to probate in all those states. Probate is a public court process, meaning if someone really wanted to, they could find out what kind of assets you were passing on when you died. If you're not a celebrity, chances are no one would care to look. However, there have been instances where people actually "work" probate records in search of people who will be inheriting assets (Creative Planning Legal Department 2021). If your assets are owned in trust, those assets are not a part of the public process.

As with most things, there is not a one-size-fits-all answer here. You may choose to add a trust to your estate plan if you have substantial assets, are single or divorced, own a business, or simply prefer the privacy. Alternatively, you may choose to create a trust in your will that takes effect at your death if your kids are under the age brackets that you define.

THE LOGISTICS

Now that you know the parts of an estate plan and have discussed who you want to list as guardians or powerholders, how do you make it official? Legal documents are drafted by attorneys, so you will need to find one. You could ask around for recommendations (If you know any financial planners or accountants, they probably have some ideas of who to talk to). You can also search websites for estate planning attorneys in your area; The National Association of Estate Planners and Councils' website and the American Academy of Estate Planning Attorneys are great places to start. There are also a lot of online options available. If you go that route, make sure you complete all the steps (like getting it notarized) to make it official.

What does it cost? That depends on a lot of factors—where you live, the attorney's hourly rate, how complicated your estate is, what documents it includes, etc. A ballpark cost for a will-based plan package that includes a will, the powers of attorney documents, and advanced directive, your cost (for the couple) would likely be in the $800 to $1,200 range. If you incorporate a revocable living trust into the mix, your total would likely be in the $2,500 to $5,000 range.

WHAT HAPPENS IF YOU DIE WITHOUT A WILL?

"Sixty-eight percent of Americans do not have a will."
—CARING.COM 2021 WILLS AND ESTATE PLANNING STUDY

If you pass away and do not have a will, this is called dying "intestate." So, any assets you own that would normally pass through a will would be distributed according to your state's intestate succession laws. This could include bank or investment accounts that are in your name only, your car, your house, or anything you own that does not have another owner or beneficiary designation.

Assets you own that have named beneficiaries will pass directly to those beneficiaries (even if you don't have a will), and those include 401(k)s, IRAs, life insurance, etc. (assuming you've named beneficiaries for them). It is best to check these designations every year for accuracy. If you listed your ex-husband as a beneficiary and never changed the designation after the divorce, he would still inherit your account. If you listed your sister as beneficiary, but the two of you haven't talked in over ten years, she will still inherit the account. Also, any assets you have transferred into a trust or where you have a payable on death (POD) or transfer on death (TOD) designation would be exempt from these intestacy rules.

Most people believe their property will automatically pass to their spouse, but under many intestacy laws, this is not the case. In some states, the spouse may only be entitled as little as one-third of the estate. Here's what the intestacy laws in Kansas are as I write this:

FOR EXAMPLE—IF YOU LIVE IN KANSAS AND DIE WITHOUT A WILL

- If you have a spouse and children, your spouse will inherit half of your intestate property and your children would inherit the other half.

(Note: This is generally not how people desire their assets to transfer. They typically want the spouse to inherit and control the assets and then have them pass to the children when the second spouse dies).

- If you have children but are not married, then the kids get everything.

(This is, of course, a problem if you have a long-time partner you would like to support).

- If you have a spouse and no kids, the spouse gets everything.
- If your parents are living and you have no spouse or children, your parents get everything.
- If you have living siblings, but no spouse, kids, or living parents, your siblings get everything.

According to Summer Ott Dierks, owner and managing partner at Dierks Law Firm, those who die without a will can cause a tremendous amount of strain and legal work for those they leave behind. She cited several examples of the extra steps that must be taken to access the deceased spouse's assets when this occurs. In the case of dying without a will in Kansas, if you have a spouse and children, then your assets are divided equally between your spouse and kids. Let's say, for example, a husband (Kansas resident) dies in a motorcycle accident, leaving behind a wife, two small kids, and one unborn child. His wife would *not* inherit all his assets to use to support her and the family. She would have to get a court-appointed conservatorship to manage the kids' half of the money. This would include managing three separate trusts for the three children until they are old enough to manage it themselves. She would have to pay legal and court fees to get all these things established.

Dierks also pointed out having property owned in multiple states or owning a business makes having an estate plan even more critical. When multiple states are involved, you must file with all the states involved and may have creditors coming for a piece of the estate from several directions. Business owners have a lot of nuances to consider. If the surviving spouse inherits the business, can they keep it running? Are they qualified to operate it (professional designations, etc.)? Are there business partners involved? What if they need to sell it to fund their spending needs?

DON'T BE LIKE THE DRAGON TATTOO GUY.

Do you remember the book *The Girl with the Dragon Tattoo*? Stieg Larsson, the guy who wrote it, passed away in 2004. He died without a will, so Swedish law decided how his assets would pass. The intestacy laws determined his entire estate should be divvied up between his father and brother. His partner of thirty-two years, Eva, received nothing. She requested the rights to control his work so it could be presented in the way he wanted. Eva was in possession of a laptop that contained partially finished versions of his work. She was not able to publish it because she does not have the rights to it. Eva claimed Steig was estranged from his father and brother and hadn't even met his brother's children. After a long dispute over the estate, Eva was allowed to keep the home she shared with Steig, but little else.

Lots of famous people have died without a will—Prince, Aretha Franklin, Michael Jackson (Although they found his eventually, it was too late.), Martin Luther King Jr., Tupac Shakur, and Chadwick Boseman. Stories of their family feuds and unresolved estates fill our social media news feeds. Some of these cases drag on for decades and take millions of dollars in legal fees to get worked out. You may not be on the same level as Tupac, but your family is complicated and unique and might not fit into the box the state intestacy laws create for you. Maybe you have a child, but you and your partner decided not to get married or are not allowed to get married in your state. Maybe you have been married several times and have two sets of stepchildren in addition to your biological children. Everyone's story is different, and you are in charge of how your story plays out.

GET YOUR ESTATE PLAN IN PLACE.

Do your loved ones a favor and put a plan in place to care of them if you are no longer around. Do not leave these important decisions up to the state; make sure you take care of your family by getting your estate plan in order.

Once the estate plan is in place, don't "set it and forget it." Review it every one to three years to be sure the people you nominated as guardians and power holders are still who you'd want to put in charge. Also, re-evaluate the documents if you are going through a major life change, like a divorce, a move, adding more kids to the family, caring for an aging parent, etc.*

*Note: I am not an attorney; consult legal counsel before making these decisions.

FAMILY EMERGENCY BINDER

If you passed away suddenly, would your spouse know the password to your phone, what bills are on autopay, and what company the life insurance is through? Usually, one person in a couple handles most of the finances and other household items, and if you are reading this book, it is probably you. Chelsea Brennan, founder of Smart Money Mamas, suggests having a family emergency binder to help your family figure out what to do next if you are hospitalized or no longer around. This binder can include passwords, information on where financial accounts and insurance policies are held, an emergency contact list, and healthcare information. Chelsea also suggests having a section with caregiving instructions. This would include information on your children's allergies, likes and dislikes, bedtime routines, babysitters, and daycare providers. You can purchase a template for this binder on her website, SmartMoneyMamas.com.

"MONEY BOSS" SYSTEMS FOR SUCCESS SUMMARY—CHAPTER 5

- As a parent, you *need* a will.
- Name guardians for your children in your will. If you don't, the court gets to decide. It's best to list your first choice and a couple of backups.
- You should have power of attorney documents in place to name decision makers if you are incapacitated.
- Once your estate plan is in place, review it every one to three years or as things change (divorce, births, etc.) to make sure it still reflects your wishes.
- Consider creating a "family emergency binder" to help your family get organized and know where things are in case of an emergency.

CHAPTER 6

THE RETIREMENT POGO STICK

———

*"The best way to predict the future
is to create the one you want."*

—BOLA SOKUNBI, FOUNDER AND CEO
OF CLEVER GIRL FINANCE

I distinctly remember the day I learned one of my friends owned a minivan. We were meeting for coffee, and she came rolling up in that unsightly loaf of bread on wheels. I was flabbergasted. *How could she do this? Has she given up on life?* Sure, both of our mothers drove minivans, but they were old, so it made sense. I teased her relentlessly and vowed I would never, *ever* drive a minivan. Fast forward seven or so years and several offspring later, and I, too, fell prey to the allure of the minivan. I was seduced by the sliding doors, multiple car seat attachments, and countless cupholders. I posed for pictures beside 2017 Toyota Siennas in the various color options. I posted the photos on Facebook for my friends to vote between Celestial Silver, Blizzard Pearl, or Crème Brûlée.

Time flies, my friends.

I know what you are thinking. Retirement is over twenty years away, how can I be thinking of that when I have so many other things to worry about now? Today we are lusting over minivans, and tomorrow we will be playing Parcheesi in rocking chairs on the patio. Retirement will be here before we know it. The truth is, the sooner you start thinking about retirement and planning for it, the more flexibility and options you'll have when the day comes.

I purposely put the retirement chapter *before* the one about college funding. As parents, we are constantly bombarded with statistics on how expensive college is and how tuition is increasing at an astronomical rate. So many young families tend to focus on saving for education expenses for the kids, putting their retirement savings on hold and in jeopardy. You should focus first on making sure your retirement savings are on track and *then* start saving for education. Your kids can work through school or get a student loans to pay for college. You can't get a loan for retirement. Sure, maybe the kids will let you move in with them during retirement, but that is not a sound financial plan (or good for family morale, for that matter).

ACHIEVING FINANCIAL INDEPENDENCE

Retirement is not about leaving your nine-to-five job and doing nothing. It is about gaining your *financial* independence and making time for your priorities and the things you value most.

Financial independence is the point when you no longer work because you *have* to; you're doing it because you *choose* to. Many people don't want to retire and sit in a rocking chair all day. They want to work a less strenuous schedule but still do some kind of work or activity they feel is interesting and meaningful. Maybe it's part-time work, starting a business, consulting, writing books, or serving on the board of a charity. Those things are still work, but they are work on your terms, not someone else's.

The goal could be spending more time with the grandkids, gardening, traveling, or just having more fun. The key is you have set yourself up to be in the position to be able to choose by being financially independent.

THE POWER OF COMPOUND INTEREST

"Compound interest is the eighth wonder of the world. He who understands it, earns it; he who doesn't, pays it."
—ALBERT EINSTEIN

To achieve financial independence, you need to start planning well in advance of your retirement date. This is why we are talking now, my friends! When retirement is far away is the best time to start planning because time is on your side. The time value of money is a truly amazing concept. The sooner you put your money to work, the more you will have down the road.

In this example, both Priya and Damon earn an annual salary of $100,000, and they happen to be in the same book club. Priya is age thirty-five and Damon is age forty-five when they start reading *Money Boss Mom*. They are inspired to start contributing 10 percent of their income to their 401(k)s immediately and do so until age sixty-five. For this example, I assume a 7 percent annual return compounded monthly. Priya, being younger, has more time on her side for compound interest to work its magic. She ends up with more than double the amount Damon has at age sixty-five.

Power of Compounding

Investor	Percent Contributed	Years Contributing	Balance at age 65
Priya	10%	Age 35–65 (30 years)	$1,016,642
Damon	10%	Age 45–65 (20 years)	$434,105

Note: There are other factors at play—inflation, company match contributions, and increases in salary, but I am trying to keep it simple here.

The average person is liable to spend up to one-third (i.e., over thirty years) of their life in retirement. That is a lot of time to plan for. The moral of the story is the sooner you start, the better off you'll be.

"Wealth is not about having a lot of money; it's about having a lot of options."

—CHRIS ROCK

NAVIGATING WHERE TO SAVE FOR RETIREMENT

We hear all the time we should be "saving for retirement." Then we are faced with an alphabet soup of various types of retirement plans, we get overwhelmed, and then we do nothing different from what we are doing now. There are many options for retirement savings that have different tax advantages. You can save through your employer's retirement plan, your own accounts outside of work, or both. This section will provide some definitions to help you sort through the noise and recognize which plans are available to you.

STEP 1—FIND OUT WHAT IS AVAILABLE THROUGH YOUR EMPLOYER AND TAKE ADVANTAGE OF IT.

Participating in whatever retirement savings plan is offered by your employer is generally the easiest place to start. The most commonly offered plan is a 401(k). If you work for the government, a school system, charitable organization, or hospital, your employer's plan is probably called a 403(b), 457 plan, or Thrift Savings Plan (TSP). If you work for a very small firm, they may offer something called a SIMPLE IRA. They all have different names but essentially accomplish the same goal of allowing employees the opportunity to direct some of their paycheck into a retirement savings vehicle. Many of those plans also include a company match or employer contribution—i.e., free money.

The beauty of employer-sponsored plans is the savings are automated for you. The contribution comes out of your paycheck and goes into the plan without you ever seeing it, so you don't have to think about savings. It just happens. Remember your "inner elephant" from chapter one? This is the part of you that steers you toward the path of least resistance. Make retirement savings easy; make it automatic.

STEP 2—EXPLORE OTHER SAVINGS OPTIONS THAT CAN BE SET UP ON YOUR OWN.

IRA—IRA stands for "individual retirement account." An IRA can be set up on your own online or with an advisor through companies like Schwab, Fidelity, Vanguard, and countless others. The IRS sets limits each year on how much a person can contribute to an IRA. These limits tend to be much lower than what you can put into a 401(k) or other employer-sponsored plan each year.

ROTH VS. TRADITIONAL

The financial industry is notorious for overloading people with confusing jargon and acronyms. "Roth" and "traditional" are terms you hear getting thrown around a lot. They basically just tell you the tax treatment of the account. These apply to IRAs but are options in a lot of company retirement plans—401(k), 403(b), etc.—as well. For example, there are

Roth IRAs and traditional IRAs, regular (traditional) 401(k) s and Roth 401(k)s.

Traditional means "pre-tax" or "tax-deferred." So, if you are making traditional contributions to a 401(k), that money has never been taxed. Your employer puts it straight into your 401(k) account, which effectively lowers your taxable income now. For example, if your paycheck is $2,500 before taxes, but $500 of it goes to your 401(k), you are only charged taxes on the $2,000 today. These dollars grow tax-deferred, meaning no tax is assessed until you withdraw the funds down the road. If you are making contributions to a traditional IRA, you may qualify for a deduction on your tax return if you are below the income limits for the year. Basically, you are saving taxes today but will owe them at some point in the future.

Roth means "after-tax" or "tax-free." If you are making Roth contributions to your 401(k), your paycheck is taxed first, then your employer deposits your contribution into the account. To compare to the previous example, if your paycheck is $2,500 before taxes, you pay taxes on that full amount, then your $500 contribution goes into the Roth 401(k). Come retirement, your withdrawals will be tax-free, including the profits you've earned. Same with a Roth IRA. You deposit after-tax funds into your Roth IRA, then they grow tax free forever. So, you pay taxes on the funds now as opposed to in the future.

Not everyone can contribute to a Roth IRA. If you make over a certain income level (set by the IRS each year), you do not qualify. There is a loophole though—the "backdoor Roth" contribution. If you make too much money to contribute to a Roth, you can still build up Roth dollars in a roundabout fashion. You can contribute funds to a traditional IRA, then convert them to a Roth. There are potential tax consequences here, so make sure you know your stuff before making this move. Generally, if you have a balance in a traditional IRA already, the backdoor Roth is not a good option for you. Work with a tax professional or financial planner to determine if this makes sense in your plan. If your employer offers a Roth 401(k), you are allowed to participate regardless of your income level.

"To Roth or not to Roth, that is the question."
—MICHAEL KITCES, FINANCIAL GURU, AUTHOR OF
THE NERD'S EYE VIEW BLOG, HEAD OF PLANNING
STRATEGY AT BUCKINGHAM WEALTH PARTNERS.

When deciding which type of account is right for you, you must consider current versus future tax rates. Basically, you want to pay taxes when the rates are lowest. So, if you are a young employee with low earnings, it is likely your tax rate will go up in the future when you grow your income. In that case, you could take advantage of lower tax rates now and do the Roth. If you are a high earner now but expect your taxable income will be much lower in retirement, it might make the most sense to do traditional contributions now.

It doesn't have to be one or the other; you can have both. You can have a traditional 401(k) and a Roth IRA on the side (if you are under the income limits and/or are doing the "backdoor Roth" contribution mentioned above).

HOW MUCH SHOULD I CONTRIBUTE?

Your target should be saving 10 to 15 percent of your income for retirement. If you are not doing any amount now, start small and work your way up to it. At the very least, contribute enough to get the maximum match from your employer. Don't walk away from free money. I suggest increasing your contributions 1 to 2 percent a year as you get pay increases until you can get to that 10 to 15 percent range or until you hit the maximum limits the IRS sets each year. Even a modest increase in contributions can make a big difference in the long run.

Look at the potential growth of these 2 percent contribution increases in the hypothetical account of an employee who earns $40,000 per year, assuming an average annual rate of return of 7 percent compounded monthly.

Retirement Contribution Rate Comparison

If You Contribute...	2%	4%	6%	8%
Monthly Contribution (approximate)	$ 66	$ 133	$ 200	$ 266
Annual Contribution (approximate)	$ 800	$ 1,600	$ 2,400	$ 3,200
In 10 Years, You Could Have...	$ 11,490	$ 23,154	$ 34,818	$ 46,309
In 20 Years, You Could Have...	$ 34,581	$ 69,687	$ 104,793	$ 139,374
In 30 Years, You Could Have...	$ 80,987	$ 163,202	$ 245,417	$ 326,405

These figures do not include a company match or annual increases in pay, so they would likely be even higher in real life.

The 10 to 15 percent of income doesn't have to all go into your company retirement plan. You could be saving a portion of that outside of work into a Roth IRA or non-retirement investment account.

WHAT IF THE MARKET CRASHES?

"Stocks are the only asset that when it doubles in price, we want to buy more of it, and when it's on sale, we don't want to buy it at all."
—LAURA ROTTER CFA, CFP®, TRUE ABUNDANCE ADVISORS

Market ebbs and flows are normal, and you should expect them instead of fearing them. Even when the value of your holdings fluctuates, regularly adding to an account designed for a long-term goal may cushion the emotional impact of market swings. If losses are offset even in part by new savings, the bottom-line number on your statement might not be quite so discouraging.

This type of savings is called "dollar-cost averaging," which is defined as investing a specific amount regularly regardless of the fluctuating price levels. You may be getting a bargain by continuing to buy (contribute) when prices are down. Dollar-cost averaging loses much of its benefit if you stop contributing when prices are reduced. In other words, stay the course. You are not retiring tomorrow; this is a long-term play. Train yourself not to react with short-term thinking.

THE RETIREMENT POGO STICK

When I was in school, they used the analogy of a three-legged stool for funding retirement spending needs. The legs of the stool indicated people could count on a combination of social security benefits, their personal savings, and a company pension plan to fund their retirement lifestyle. Now, that three-legged stool is more like a pogo stick. Pensions are being frozen or discontinued, and the long-term fate of the social security system as we know it is yet to be determined. Odds are you will still get a social security benefit in some form, but it will only replace a small percentage of your current income. That leaves your personal savings to pick up all the slack. Now more than ever, your financial independence is directly correlated to your ability to save a portion of the income you have now.

"Consistency breeds success. If you develop good habits and apply them consistently—through bull and bear markets— you'll be successful."
—RON CARSON, TESTED IN THE TRENCHES

IS SOCIAL SECURITY A PONZI SCHEME?

When FDR rolled out the social security system in 1935, benefits would be paid to retirees over age sixty-five. The funny thing is for a person born in 1935, the average life expectancy for a man was sixty and a woman was sixty-four. Those numbers are somewhat skewed because of infant mortality rates and childhood diseases, but you can make the argument they didn't expect people to collect benefits for long. The basic set up was for the current working generation to pay into the system and finance the retired generation's monthly allowance. What could go wrong?

People are now living much longer and having fewer children, so the younger generations are now smaller in numbers than the older ones. That brings me back to the original question: is social security a Ponzi scheme? The short answer is "no," but there are some parallels. Webster's Dictionary definition of a Ponzi scheme is "a form of fraud in which belief in the success of a nonexistent enterprise is fostered by the payment of quick returns to the first investors from money invested by later investors." Social security is not hiding anything. All their cash flow numbers, balances, and problems are a matter of public record, so it's not technically being fraudulent by any stretch. However, the way the system's success relies on "future investors" contributing does feel borderline Ponzi-*ish*.

I do believe social security will still exist when our generation retires, but it will look different than it does today. There are countless proposals out there on how to keep social security solvent. Many of them include a combination of increasing the full retirement age, expanding the income that is subject to the tax, increasing the payroll tax rate, or making changes to how they index longevity and the cost-of-living adjustment. The moral of the story is social security will likely be a part of your retirement plan, but not a big part.

WHAT SHOULD I DO WITH MY 401(K) WHEN I LEAVE A JOB?

According to a January 2018 report from the Bureau of Labor Statistics, the average person changes jobs ten to fifteen times during their career. Most of the time, workers spend five years or fewer in each job. If you participated in the company retirement plan at each of those jobs (which would be a good idea), you might have ten to fifteen accounts floating out there with different providers by the time you retire. You have some options, though. You could roll it into an IRA, roll it into your new company plan, or leave it where it is. Here are some pros and cons of each option:

Some pros of rolling it into an IRA include flexibility in investment options since you are no longer limited by the choices within the 401(k) plan. Lower fees—401(k) plans typically have higher fees than IRAs because they cost more to maintain (though this is not always the case). It could simplify your life in some capacity. If you have worked at six different places in your career and rolled them all into the same IRA, you have one account to track, not six. If you were to roll it into your new company plan, that keeps things simple as well, since there are fewer accounts to keep track of. Another benefit here is, if you have rolled all your old company plans into your current one and do not maintain an IRA balance, you may be a good candidate for a "backdoor Roth" contribution, even if you make too much income to qualify for a Roth. If you have an IRA balance, the backdoor Roth strategy is less attractive. Assets in 401(k)s typically have better creditor protection in bankruptcy and other legal matters. If you are at risk of legal issues, it may be best to keep them in the 401(k) umbrella. IRAs are protected in legal matters as well, but via state laws, which vary.

Notice I didn't include "cash it out" as an option. That is generally a terrible idea. If you are under fifty-nine-and-a-half years old and cash out your 401(k), you will lose almost half of it (depending on your tax bracket) to taxes and penalties. For example, let's say you are forty-six years old and making a career change. Your oldest is starting college next year, so you decide to cash out your $20,000 401(k) to help pay those expenses. You are in the 25 percent federal bracket, your state tax is 5 percent, and the penalty tax is an additional 10 percent on top of that. You would take a 40 percent cut on that deal and only end up with $12,000 in your pocket. Some plans do allow withdrawals without the penalty if you have left the employer and are fifty-five or older.

There are no one-size-fits-all solutions here, so it is best to evaluate your overall situation and get some help from a professional to choose the best course of action.

SO, WHAT DO I DO NOW?

Try to sock away at least 10 to 15 percent of your income each year in retirement savings. Utilize your employer's 401(k), 403(b), or 457 plans to build up long-term retirement savings that are invested for your future. Work toward maximizing the amount you contribute to these plans and pay attention to age-related catch-up provisions. The catch-up just means you get to contribute more once you are age fifty and above. Do not miss out on that employer match; remember that is *free money.* The more you contribute now, the longer the funds can grow.

Don't have an employer plan to contribute to? Work with an accountant and a financial planner to figure out the best savings vehicle for your situation. As we discussed in chapter three, the best way to start building any savings or investment balance is to make the contributions automatic. You essentially want to make your savings and investments like a bill that is paid automatically each month. This is a way to force the "pay yourself first" mentality. You force the savings and make it automatic so you don't just spend those dollars as you might if they were just sitting in your bank account.

"MONEY BOSS" SYSTEMS FOR SUCCESS SUMMARY—CHAPTER 6

- Automate your retirement savings to make it easy on your inner elephant.
- Aim to get up to 10 to 15 percent of your income going into investments for retirement.
- If a company retirement plan—401(k), 403(b), 457, etc.—is available to you, take advantage of it.
- Make sure you are contributing enough to get the full match from your employer and do 1 to 2 percent increases every year until you get up to the 10 to 15 percent contribution target.

CHAPTER 7

INVESTING SHOULD BE BORING

———

*"It's ironic that people are afraid of 'possibly'
losing money in the stock market, when they will
certainly run out of money if they don't invest."*

—RAMIT SETHI, AUTHOR OF I WILL
TEACH YOU TO BE RICH

Millennials are doing a lot of things right. This generation is known for being collaborative, positive, and for seeking out opportunities to make the world a better place. We question the status quo, stand up for the little guy, and want to do work that is meaningful. High fives all around! Here is the bad news: a large chunk of the millennial generation is making a *huge* mistake that will cost them big time.

According to a study by GOBankingRates in 2019, 43 percent of millennials are not investing their money. That means just under half of this generation is not taking advantage of a significant means of accumulating wealth. When you are investing, your funds are growing for you without you having to do a thing. You are essentially making money while you sleep. So, why are so many young Americans making this major financial mistake?

There could be lots of reasons. Millennials are kids of crisis. We came of age in the dot-com bubble of the early 2000s and the Great Recession of 2008–2009. We've seen the market crash, banks fail, and people we love suffer foreclosures and job loss. Millennials are known for having large amounts of student loan debt, so many of them feel they don't have the funds to be able to invest. Others are scared and don't know what to do, so they do nothing. They ignore the problem and just hope it goes away—not a solid strategy.

You have already learned in chapter two that compounding interest and the time value of money are your best friend. The sooner you get moving, the better. The longer you wait to start investing, the more money you stand to lose in your lifetime. Let's turn this train around.

HOW DO I KNOW WHAT I SHOULD BE INVESTING IN?

There are a lot of factors to consider when choosing how your funds should be invested. Your age, your time horizon (when you'll need the funds for spending), your goals, and your appetite for risk should be factored into the equation. Generally, you want to make sure your cash balances are adequate, and then you can invest any funds you have above that amount. In other words, you want to be sure you have enough cash socked away in an emergency fund to cover three to six months' worth of expenses (which we covered in chapter two). Then, you will want to consider any other big spending items in the next eighteen to twenty-four months. If you plan to purchase a car soon, make a down payment on a house, do a remodel, etc., those funds should stay in cash as well. Anything above that amount, you can put to work.

WHERE SHOULD I PUT MY EGGS?

We have all heard the phrase, "Don't put all of your eggs in one basket," but what does that really mean? Well, if you put all your eggs in one basket and then drop the basket, you will lose all your eggs. Similarly, if you invest all your money in one company stock or single asset class, and that company fails or that asset class underperforms, you have "lost" all your money. In the investment world, this problem is solved through diversification and managing the risk exposure in your portfolio.

HOW MANY EGGS GO IN WHICH BASKETS?

Asset allocation is the first step in creating a diversified investment portfolio. Asset allocation means deciding how your investment dollars should be distributed among broad asset classes, such as stocks, bonds, and cash equivalents.

There are also alternative investments that don't fall in those broad categories, like gold, real estate, cryptocurrency, private equity, art, antiques, etc. Diversifying your investment mix amongst the various asset classes is a key tool for managing market volatility. Because asset classes often perform differently depending on market conditions, spreading your assets among them has the potential to help reduce your overall risk exposure. For instance, your stocks may go down while your bonds go up, or vice versa.

Some broad terms that get thrown around are "equity" and "fixed income." An equity investment is money invested in a company by purchasing shares of that company in the stock market. It can be owning a stock outright (like owning shares of Apple stock) or owning a mutual fund that is a basket of several different stocks. The equity side adds growth, but also risk, to the portfolio. When the market is doing well, these underlying company values may be high, increasing the value of your investment. When the market is down (like during the Great Recession of 2008–2009 or the lockdown days of the COVID-19 pandemic), company values, as well as your investment value, may go down. When you hear the word "equity" when talking about investments, it is a general reference for stocks, or investments that contain or track stocks.

Fixed income investments serve as a buffer against market fluctuations. It is the "steady-eddie" side of the equation. These investments don't give much in terms of return or gains, but they don't go down as much either. These are typically bond holdings that pay a known interest rate to the investor for a period of time. What is a bond? A bond is a debt instrument where you, as the investor, are essentially loaning money to a borrower—usually the government or a corporation. This loan has a maturity date and interest rate. As the bond investor, you are paid interest payments by the borrowing entity over the life of the loan (i.e., until the maturity date or when you sell the bond). At the maturity date, you get your initial investment back as well. Your overall allocation to fixed income should generally increase as you age or as your tolerance for risk declines.

So how much do you put in each basket? If you have too much allocated to cash, then you run the risk of losing money to inflation. If you have too much allocated to stocks, you may be losing sleep at night dealing with the daily fluctuations of the market. Too much in fixed income could mean you are missing out on returns and damaging the long-term growth in your portfolio. The answer is different for everyone. You need to consider your tolerance for risk, your financial resources, your long-term goals, and your investment timeframe to figure out the appropriate mix for you.

ALLOCATION RULES OF THUMB

The old rule of thumb used to be that you should subtract your age from one hundred and that is the percentage of your portfolio you should keep in stocks or equity investments. For example, if you're thirty, you should keep 70 percent of your portfolio in equities. If you're seventy, you should keep 30 percent of your portfolio in equities.

However, with Americans living longer and longer, the rule has evolved to taking one hundred and twenty minus your age. This is because if you need to make your money last longer, you'll need the extra growth that stocks can provide. Under those rules, a thirty-year-old should have 90 percent in equities and a seventy-year-old should have 50 percent in equities.

INVESTING SHOULD BE BORING

Plain oatmeal is an incredibly bland choice for breakfast, but it is good for you and gets the job done. You would much rather have the Denny's Grand Slam Slugger breakfast with pancakes, eggs, hash browns, bread, sausage, *and* bacon, but with that comes heartburn, saturated fat, and more calories than a human should consume in one meal. It is not sustainable. If you ate that every day, you would likely be overweight, have cholesterol that was through the roof, and have a shortened life span with a side of diabetes. Choosing the less exciting choice is generally better when it comes to your investment strategy as well. It brings less heartburn and is better for the long-term outlook of your assets.

"Eighty-three percent of the wealthy say their largest investment gains have come from smaller wins over time rather than taking big risks."
—RAMIT SETHI, I WILL TEACH YOU TO BE RICH

If you are buying a stock on Monday, watching it every waking second, and selling it for a five-dollar gain on Thursday, you are not investing; you are day-trading. If what you are doing is some sort of game influenced by fun banter, social media posts, and bets with your buddies, you are not investing; you are speculating. Buying one stock with the hope of making a quick buck is a gamble. You are betting on that company doing well in the short term. You are speculating (making an educated guess) that the risk is worth it. Day-trading and speculation are both fine in small doses. The key is anything you gamble with should be funds you are okay losing. Maybe it's your $2,000 bonus that is purely excess. You don't need it for spending or paying off debt, your emergency fund is full, and your savings goals are on track, so you want to use it as "play money." Your retirement portfolio should not be something you gamble with. Your long-term investment strategy should be *boring*, like oatmeal.

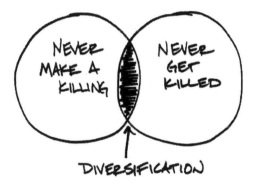

This is one of many great graphics by Carl Richards at the Behavior Gap.

Here's an example. Maverick is forty and just did the rule of thumb calculation, indicating he should have 80 percent of his portfolio in equities. What now? Buy a bunch of shares of Tesla and let it ride? Put it all in cryptocurrency? That's a negative, Ghost Rider. Buying individual stocks isn't necessarily a bad idea. They can be great if you have the time, knowledge, resources, and desire to do it right. Most Americans do not. Maverick should keep it simple. By investing in index funds, ETFs, or mutual funds, he has access to an already diversified portfolio at a lower cost and less risk.

QUICK DEFINITIONS OF SOME "BORING" (GOOD) INVESTMENT OPTIONS

MUTUAL FUND

A basket of stocks, bonds, or other assets operated by a professional money manager. Mutual funds give small investors access to professionally managed portfolios at a lower price. Each shareholder that owns a mutual fund participates in the gains and losses of the fund.

INDEX FUND

Essentially, this is a mutual fund designed to mimic the components and performance of a market index, like the S&P 500. Index funds provide broad market exposure with low operating expenses, so they are very accessible to small investors. An index fund will never perform better than the index it is tracking. This is a passive strategy where you are participating in the gains of the market but not trying to beat it.

EXCHANGE-TRADED FUND (ETF)

This is similar to mutual funds and index funds in that it tracks an index, sector, or other asset, but it can be traded on the stock exchange the same as a regular stock. This means its share price fluctuates throughout the day as the ETF is bought and sold over the course of the day. This is different from mutual funds, which only trade once per day after the market closes. ETFs offer lower expense ratios than buying stocks individually.

A mutual fund or index fund is a basket of multiple stocks, so the daily market swings aren't as volatile. For instance, the S&P 500 index represents five hundred different large company stocks in the US. Most mutual funds hold over one hundred individual stocks. Billionaire investor Warren Buffett has been quoted saying an S&P 500 index fund is the best investment most Americans can make. He added that he wants his own wife's money invested in such a fund after he's gone. So, Maverick—from the previous example—could choose to put 80 percent of his investments in an S&P 500 index fund and 20 percent into a bond fund. If he wanted to add some international holdings, he could reduce the amount of the equity in the S&P and do a percentage toward an international index fund.

Mutual funds, index funds, and ETFs are great, affordable ways for the everyday investor to have access to the market. They offer low expense ratios, are less volatile, and are easier to maintain than owning stocks outright.

401(k) plans generally offer target-date funds that make investing super easy. You plug in your retirement date and the fund automatically gets more conservative as you get older. Note: make sure you look into the allocation within the funds as you may choose a date beyond when you actually plan to retire. This is because they can get too conservative too quickly and leave you with too low of a percentage on the equity side.

WHAT DIVERSIFICATION IS NOT

Spreading your assets amongst several different investment advisors or brokerage houses is *not* an effective diversification strategy, especially if all those accounts contain similar holdings. For instance, if you use three different brokerage firms to house your investments, and they all invest in large cap stocks, your eggs are still in the same basket. If you own stocks in five different big tech firms, your eggs are still all in one basket.

In my interview with Nick Raich, CEO of The Earnings Scout, he confirmed boring is better for the long term. He spoke in baseball references and said when you're always looking for big wins and swinging for the fences, you're likely to strike out more often than you get a homerun. He suggested you should just "get on base" and start investing in the simple stuff. Singles and doubles will add up to wins over time.

Your cubicle at work is right between Exciting Eric and Mundane Mike. Eric loves to talk about what he's invested in— mostly big tech, cryptocurrency, or stocks that are trending.

He spends a lot of his day tracking stock prices and sharing screenshots of his "wins" on social media. It's always exciting to hear how he plans to invest the next stimulus check and what buys and sells he did today. Mundane Mike is pretty quiet about his investment strategy because there really isn't much to say. He consistently saves and invests 10 percent of his earnings and is invested for the long term. No huge daily wins (or losses) to report, just steadily growing over time.

Be like Mike. Stick to simple basics and choose low-cost, "boring" investments to diversify your holdings. Alternatively, you could hire a financial advisor whom you trust to figure out the best place to put your proverbial eggs. Working with a professional does generally cost more than investing in an index fund on your own. As it should; you are hiring an expert, and they should be paid for their work. Just be sure you understand your advisor's philosophy, how they are choosing the investments, and how they are compensated.

"Clever girls know...investing is an essential part of being able to achieve the big financial goals you have for your life."
—BOLA SOKUNBI, FOUNDER AND CEO
OF CLEVER GIRL FINANCE

I DON'T WANT TO LOSE MONEY WHEN THE MARKET SWINGS

People often say they have "lost money" when the market goes down. This is not an accurate statement. You have not lost money when the market goes down. You own the same number of shares as you did before; they just have less value.

If you sell the shares, you capture that loss and make it real. If you stay the course and ride it out, the shares have the opportunity to bounce back and continue to grow.

Here's an example: Dominic and Darla are twins who both turned twenty-eight on March 23, 2020. This happened to be the day the market took a big nosedive due to uncertainty during the COVID-19 pandemic. A few years ago, for their twenty-fifth birthdays, they had opened up Roth IRAs with the $1,000 they each received from Grandma Nell. Being twins, they love doing things together, so they both invested in an S&P 500 index fund and enjoyed watching it grow to $1,350.

By March 23, 2020, the S&P index had fallen 34 percent, bringing the value of their respective investments down to $851. Dominic jumped on the fear bandwagon and decided to sell the S&P fund and move to cash until things "settle down." Darla considered selling but decided to take a bigger picture approach. She knows the Roth IRA is for her retirement, which is over thirty years away, so she decided to stay invested. On March 24, 2020 (the very next day), the S&P 500 rose 9.4 percent, the biggest one-day gain since 2008. Dominic kept his Roth in cash for the rest of 2020 because it felt like the economy was in ruins. Darla left hers invested and stayed the course. The S&P index ended up with a positive 16 percent return for 2020 even though the world was in crisis. On December 31, 2020, Darla had $1,566 in her account, and Dominic was still at $851.

"Humans are wired to act; markets tend to reward inaction."

—DANIEL CROSBY, THE BEHAVIORAL INVESTOR

KEEPING DOWN MARKETS IN PERSPECTIVE

I don't have to tell you the stock market is volatile; you already know that. As humans, we are wired for a fight or flight response when we sense danger. So, your first reaction in a down market might be to take the money and run, get out of the market all together, and stuff the cash under your mattress. Alternatively, your reaction might be to fight, to get aggressive, and to change your investment strategy completely. I want to share with you some facts, history, and definitions to give you some perspective as you decide how you will react during turbulent times.

I have a chart in my office that shows the hypothetical growth of $10,000 invested on January 1, 1980 through March 31, 2020, as presented by the FMRCo Asset Allocation Research Team (Fidelity). The first column shows if that $10,000 was left in the market the whole time, it would be worth $697,421 on March 31, 2020. Think about all the terrible market events that happened during the time frame of 1980 to 2020. The first things that come to my mind are the dot-com bubble, the September 11, 2001 terrorist attacks, Brexit, quantitative easing, the Great Recession of 2008–2009, and of course, the beginning of the COVID-19 pandemic. If you go back further into the archives, there was the Iraq War, the Chernobyl disaster, several bombings, the Gulf War, and the crash of 1987. All those terrible things happened during that time frame, but if you left those $10,000 dollars invested in the

S&P that entire time, the $10,000 would have grown to over $600,000 by March 31, 2020.

The next column shows the value of that $10,000 if the funds were taken out of the market and missed the five best days (*five days* over a whooping forty years). By missing the five best market days (which often immediately follow the worst ones), the total value is $432,411, more than $200,000 *less* than it would have been if you had just left the funds alone. This particular chart represents over 14,600 days in the market (forty years and change). The next column shows further declines if you missed the best ten days, leaving you with a balance of $313,377. That is less than half of the value you would have had if you had just left it invested for those ten days. The chart has a few more columns, but I think you see where I'm going here.

The problem with "waiting until things settle down" is the market moves ahead of the economy, so if you wait until the economy has turned around and things "feel good," then you already missed most of the returns.

Let me give you another example. If you look at our last big crisis, the market crash of 2008–2009, headlines were terrible all of 2009. It was the Great Recession, "The Big Short." Huge companies filed for bankruptcy, banks had to be bailed out, millions of people were out of work, etc. I don't have to remind you of how terrible that time felt. But if you look at the market returns from March of 2009 through December of 2009, the market was up over 70 percent. If you missed the five best days during that time, you missed half of that return. If you missed the ten best days, you only saw a 15 percent gain. According to Wikipedia, we recovered from that recession in June of 2009, but the job market still looked bleak, and most of the news was still negative at the time. As with most things, hindsight is twenty-twenty.

"You make most of your money in bear markets, you just don't realize it at the time."

—SHELBY DAVIS, DAVIS ASSET MANAGEMENT

DEFINITIONS AND FUN FACTS ABOUT THE MARKET

BULL MARKET:
A market in which share prices are rising for sustained periods of time.

BEAR MARKET:
A time of prolonged price declines when the market is down 20 percent or more from the most recent high.

A CORRECTION:
A 10 percent to 19.99 percent decline from the recent high. Corrections are actually really common; there's usually about one a year. Once you realize that, as an investor, you are less likely to react irrationally and will actually view those times as a buying opportunity.

A RECESSION:
Two down quarters in a row (six months or more).

FUN FACTS:

- Stocks lose 36 percent on average during a bear market.
- By contrast, they gain 112 percent on average during bull markets. Markets are positive the majority of the time. We just don't remember the good times as well as we remember the bad ones.
- Over a fifty-year investment time horizon, you will have seen an average of fourteen bear markets. Bear markets are pretty normal. They just don't feel good when you're in them.

Oddly enough, a lot of market returns are actually made during bear markets. Half of the S&P's strongest days in the last twenty years happened during bear markets. Another 30 percent happened in the first two months of a bull market, when it wasn't yet clear we were in a recovery.

Try not to let fear drive your investment strategy. Focus on the facts and try to keep things in perspective. Timing the market is actually very hard to do, and sometimes the best thing to do when it comes to your investments is *nothing*.

"Never underestimate the power of doing nothing."

—WINNIE THE POOH

THE EMOTIONAL SIDE OF INVESTING

"When dealing with people, remember you are not dealing with creatures of logic, but with creatures of emotion, creatures bristling with prejudice and motivated by pride and vanity."

—DALE CARNEGIE

Our emotions play a big role in our decision making whether we realize it or not. We like to think the choices we make are the result of a thoughtful, rational evaluation of the available options. In reality, we are emotional creatures who usually make decisions based on preferences, habits, and feelings. When it comes to investing, letting emotions drive our investment decisions can be detrimental to our long-term plans.

"Ninety percent of the decisions we make are based on emotion, not rational thought and measured consideration."

—DANIEL KAHNEMAN, PSYCHOLOGIST

SIMON AND XYZ

Simon purchased some XYZ stock in his early twenties, and it went nowhere but up. The gains from this stock helped him to buy cars, a house, and supplement his family income to pay for his three kids in college. Simon feels like he is a prudent, wise investor. However, he may have an unhealthy emotional attachment to this particular stock. Simon could be an investment genius, or his choice of XYZ stock could have been a stroke of dumb luck. Fast-forward thirty years and XYZ stock has been consistently down for the last ten of those years. He refuses to sell this stock and actually talks about it like it's an old friend instead of an investment tool. From a rational standpoint, it may be time for Simon to cut his losses and sell some or all the stock. Instead of diversifying, Simon decides to hold on to XYZ and "ride it out." He is making decisions purely on emotion, not facts or concrete information.

FRANCINE THE COMPANY GAL

Francine prides herself on loyalty and worked at LMNOP Company for thirty-seven amazing years. She has since retired but has extremely fond memories of her time with LMNOP, and she considers her former colleagues family. LMNOP matched all employee 401(k) contributions with LMNOP stock and offered an employee stock purchase plan to allow employees to buy the company stock at a 10 percent discount. Francine participated in both programs and now has an investment portfolio that is 47 percent LMNOP stock.

She has had several chances to diversify her holdings while working at LMNOP but felt good about owning a stock within her beloved company. Now that she is retired, there are absolutely no restrictions on the amount of LMNOP stock she can sell to diversify her portfolio. She held onto the stock, even when she heard LMNOP was offering a voluntary severance package and had laid off half of their workforce in the past few years. Francine will likely hold on to this stock even if it continues to decrease in value. After all, she can't sell out of the company that was like her family all this time!

PHUONG THE "NON-FINANCIAL" SPOUSE

Phuong is a widow who was never involved in the family finances until her husband passed away. She now must figure out where all her assets are and what she owns. Phuong knows her late husband, Fred, was a big fan of investing in silver bars and kept a large stash of them in a fire-proof safe in the basement and an even larger stash in a private company vault. He also believed accumulating cash value in a life insurance policy was a good way to invest and save money, so he had several policies on the couple in place. After a few years, cash flow became pretty tight for Phuong, and she was having a hard time paying the bills. The growing cost of the life insurance premiums and the storage fees for the silver bars were putting a strain on her finances. Phuong could sell the silver and save herself the cost of storage. She could also take the cash value of the life insurance policies and discontinue paying the hefty premiums. Phuong and Fred had never discussed how assets should be managed after he was gone, but she assumed he would want her to continue investing the way he had. In reality, I am sure Fred would want Phuong to do whatever she needed to do to live a happy, healthy, and financially stable life.

LESSONS LEARNED

You may have found yourself or someone you love in circumstances like those of Simon, Francine, or Phuong. The common thread is people often make decisions based on emotion and not rational facts. It is unrealistic to expect everyone to always be rational, but such decisions can endanger your livelihood.

I believe the problem *and* the solution are driven by emotion. Silver, too much life insurance, or the XYZ and LMNOP stocks may have all been good investments at one time, but they may not be the best going forward. What may change Simon, Francine, and Phuong's minds is a stronger emotion outweighing their existing preferences. Simon may realize he does not want the children he put through college to be supporting him for the rest of his life, so he may decide it is time to diversify out of XYZ stock. Francine may become overwhelmed with thankfulness that LMNOP provided such a great experience and income for thirty-seven years, but now she can diversify her portfolio and instead purchase her former company's products as a way to show her support. Phuong may one day wake up and realize she has no other assets and can no longer afford her home. Her fear of losing the house and not living the lifestyle to which she has become accustomed may drive her to sell the silver and discontinue the life insurance.

These stories could have a happy ending or a tragic one; it's a matter of mindset. It's important to be grateful for past fortune (or luck), but we must consider our current circumstances and future outlooks. Certain decisions may have been successful at one point in time, but they may not be the right decision now or in the future.

THREE THINGS TO KEEP IN MIND AS AN INVESTOR

1. Focus On What You Can Control

You must keep your emotions in check and focus on what you *can* control. Most of the time, you should be doing the exact opposite of what you feel like doing. You know that Warren Buffett quote, "Be greedy when others are fearful and be fearful when others are greedy."? A down market is a buying opportunity. Everything is on sale, but you don't feel like putting a bunch of money into the stock market because it is scary. Same thing on the flip side—when things are doing great, that is actually the time to trim back your holdings and move more to cash and bonds, which doesn't feel right either. You must take emotions out of the equation. Focus on keeping enough cash on hand for emergencies, automating your savings goals, and setting yourself up for success for the long haul. Don't concern yourself with short-term swings.

2. Review Your Investments in the Right Context

In a down market, you may be thinking, "My equity investments are down 10 percent. This is awful!" Well, put it in perspective. If the S&P is down 15 percent, and your large cap holdings are only down 10 percent, you are actually doing really well. Figure out how your investments are performing within their own category. Make sure you are using the right benchmarks for comparison. Most portfolios should be diversified, including some sort of mix of stocks and bonds, and within those there should be an allocation for large, mid-size, and small cap stocks as well as international and emerging equities. On the bond side, there are also different flavors that have their own benchmarks against which you can compare. The problem with talking about the "market" is the reporters are not talking about a diversified portfolio mix; they are referring to the US stock market and usually just large company stocks, which doesn't show you the whole picture. If you are using index funds, those already track their respective indexes, so your portfolio should be right in line with what the index is doing.

Let's say your 401(k) allocation is 80 percent to a domestic large company growth fund and 20 percent fixed income (bond funds). You look at your year-end return and it is 9.5 percent. You think, "Hey, that sounds pretty good!" Then you hear on the Squawk Box that the S&P return for the year was 15 percent, so what gives? Well, only 80 percent of your portfolio can be compared to the S&P, not the whole thing. That 20 percent bond portion serves as a buffer. It won't have as high of returns as the growth fund in good times, but it likely won't have as low of returns in bad times.

3. Take Another Look at Your Plan—The Big Picture

When you're stressed and overwhelmed, separating reality from all the noise you're hearing around you is tough. Looking at your comprehensive financial plan will help you get a sense of where you *really* are and can help eliminate some of the fear and anxiety weighing you down.

Remind yourself of your short-term and long-term goals as these are the *real* benchmarks for your investment strategy and the reason you're investing in the first place. How have your goals changed due to these market changes? Odds are many of your long-term goals will stay the same. If this is the case, it is often best to stick with the plan you have. Most financial plans are built with the expectation that markets ebb and flow and account for that.

Uncertain times are scary, but if you can focus on what you can control and make sure your big picture plan is on track, you'll be able to weather these storms with a lot more confidence. Data clearly states the average investor buys high, sells low, and trades frequently, which incurs taxes and cuts into returns. Be better than average; do less. Invest in boring long-term funds with the bigger picture in mind.

"MONEY BOSS" SYSTEMS FOR SUCCESS—CHAPTER 7

- Don't let your emotions drive your investment decisions.
- When it comes to investments, boring is better for the long term.
- Make sure you're using the right benchmark—your goals.
- Focus on what you can control.

CHAPTER 8

COLLEGE FUNDING

——

'We have three cats. It's like having children,
but there is no tuition involved."

—RON REAGAN

If you skipped ahead to this chapter, you need to hear this: make sure your retirement savings are started *before* you start saving for your kid's college. There are options to pay for college, but you can't get loans for retirement. Before you start a college savings fund, make sure you are contributing to your retirement accounts (ideally, at least 10 percent of your income) and your emergency cash cushion is funded (three to six months' worth of fixed expenses).

IS COLLEGE STILL WORTH IT?

With the astronomical increases in the cost of college tuition, some wonder if it is still a worthy investment. Every investment comes with a certain level of risk, but the data indicates a college education generates a good return. On average, those with a bachelor's degree earn significantly more than their peers with only a high school diploma. According to Northeastern University and the Bureau of Labor Statistics (2019), the median salary for workers with high school diplomas is $38,792, and they have an average unemployment rate of 3.7 percent. By contrast, the median salary for workers with bachelor's degrees is $64,896, and their unemployment rate is 2.2 percent on average. Trade school graduates' salaries vary widely depending on specialty and level of experience, but generally fall somewhere in between.

Many other factors come into play, of course, including what the student ends up majoring in. In Ron Lieber's book *The Price You Pay for College*, he cites the research of Douglas Webber, a professor who studies the economics of higher education. Webber concluded most science, technology, engineering, or math majors are very likely to achieve a positive return on their investment. He said arts and humanities majors paying higher tuition at private universities were less likely to see a positive return.

The Georgetown University Center on Education and the Workforce predicts that 70 percent of all jobs will require some post-high school education by 2027.

WHAT WILL IT COST AND HOW
DO FAMILIES PAY FOR IT?

According to EducationData.org, the average cost of atten-
dance for a student living on campus at a public four-year
in-state school is $25,864 a year. This represents a total cost—
not just tuition and fees, but also books, supplies, and room
and board. So, sending one child to college for a four-year
degree will cost just over $100,000. Ouch! I know it seems
like a big deal, but the truth is you are not required to pay
for your children's college education. My parents didn't pay
for mine, and I turned out alright.

Here are some stats about how college is funded from Edu-
cationData.org:

- There is enough scholarship and grant money available
  to give $9,744 to every full-time student.
- $120 billion in federal student aid goes out each year in
  the form of grants, work-study, and loans.
- Students use financial aid to pay for 92 percent of college
  costs.
- Sixty-three percent of all undergraduates receive at least
  one grant or scholarship.
- Of full-time undergraduates, 76.7 percent receive a grant
  or scholarship.

The gist is there are funds available for college, so you don't
have to foot the full bill (or any of it, for that matter). Plus,
many students can successfully hold part-time jobs to supplement their spending needs while in school. There are
also cool programs out there that make tuition free. Several

colleges are offering the opportunity to graduate debt-free in exchange for work hours. At the College of the Ozarks in Point Lookout, Missouri, each student participates in the on-campus work program for fifteen hours a week and serves two forty-hour work weeks per school year in exchange for their degree.

Rick Kahler with Kahler Financial Group actually cited that kids perform *worse* in college if the full cost was paid by their parents. He studied the research of Laura T. Hamilton and reviewed her works published in the American Sociological Review. Her study shows students whose education was funded by parents actually have lower grade point averages (GPAs) than students who worked their way through school and were responsible for some of their expenses. This goes against conventional thinking. We assume if the student doesn't have to work during school, they will have more time for their studies and perform better. This has proven to be incorrect. It turns out having "skin in the game" really does make a difference. Students who must work to pay for school (or maintain scholarships) are incentivized to work harder, manage their time better, and do well.

Take care of your retirement first—and both you and your kids may be better off for it. Whatever you do, do not take a loan or withdrawal against your 401(k) plan to pay for college. That is a lose-lose proposition. If you take a withdrawal before the age of fifty-nine and a half, you will pay significant taxes and penalties. If you're over fifty-nine and a half, you'll still owe a lot in taxes, even without the penalty. If you take a loan, there's not a penalty or taxes owed, but you do take a tax hit overall. The funds with which you repay the loan are after-tax dollars (meaning you already paid taxes on them). Then, if you turn around and put them in your 401(k), you'll pay tax again on them later when you take them out in retirement. There is no need to pay taxes twice, folks. Plus, if you take a loan and you are downsized or leave that job, the loan is due in full.

If you raid your retirement funds to pay for college, you are robbing your future self. You run the risk of running out of money once you've hung up your cleats. Taking a large chunk out of your retirement plan is really hard to recover from.

WAYS TO SAVE

529 PLANS

This is the most common choice for education savings and will probably be the one that makes sense for you. The 529 plans are great for tax benefits now and tax-free growth of your investment. Any money you put in grows tax-free as long as it's taken out for qualified education expenses. These include tuition, books, supplies, fees, and room and board. If the funds are used for anything outside of these qualified expenses, a tax penalty of 10 percent is assessed on the plan's earnings. Note this 10 percent tax applies to your *gains* in the account, not the funds that you put in—just the profit you made. The 529 funds can be used for traditional universities, community college, culinary school, technical school, cosmetology, etc.—not just four-year colleges.

As of 2018, when some new rules came out, 529 plan funds can also be used to pay for kindergarten through twelfth grade private school tuition. However, for the K–12 expenses, the funds can *only* be used for tuition, not uniforms, fees, books, etc. This was a big shift. Before 2018, 529 funds could only be used for post-high school education expenses.

There are no federal tax benefits for contributions made to 529 plans, but there may be some state tax benefits depending on where you live. Nine states currently have no income tax and therefore no deduction for 529 contributions. Alaska, Florida, Nevada, South Dakota, Texas, Washington, and Wyoming all levy no state income tax. The two others, New Hampshire and Tennessee, don't tax earned wages. Seven states currently have a state income tax but do not offer a deduction for contributions: California, Delaware, Hawaii, Kentucky, Maine, New Jersey, and North Carolina.

So, if you live in any of the other thirty-four states, you may qualify for a state tax deduction today for contributions you make. If you do live in one of those sixteen states, you don't get a deduction, but you could still benefit from tax-free growth.

Every state has a 529 plan, but you don't necessarily have to participate in your state's plan. Arizona, Arkansas, Kansas, Minnesota, Missouri, Montana, and Pennsylvania are the seven states that offer their residents tax deductions for contributions to *any* state's plan, not just their own. This is cool because you have the flexibility to choose whichever plan you want based on who has the best performance, lower fees, or any other metric that is important to you. For the other states that allow deductions, you'll want to participate in your state plan to be eligible for the tax break.

The maximum amount you can put in per year is based on the federal gifting limit that year. As I write this, that limit is $15,000 per person. So, technically, each parent could put in $15K per child into their 529 plan each year. There are ways to "superfund" a 529 plan with five years' worth of gifts at a time, but you need to work with a tax professional for that. Depending on your state, there are limits to the deduction for which you are eligible.

"What if my kid is a genius and gets a full ride and doesn't need this account?" These 529s are easy to transfer between siblings or other family members. You could change the beneficiary to a sibling, cousin, or even yourself.

COVERDELL EDUCATION SAVINGS ACCOUNTS (ESAS)—SOMETIMES CALLED AN EDUCATION IRA

This account is similar to a 529 plan from the tax standpoint but has some other rules involved. An ESA allows you to save $2,000 per year, per child, and it grows tax-free. There are income limits; if you make over a certain amount of money, you are not eligible to contribute to these types of accounts.

The Coverdell can be applied for any higher education and K–12 education expenses. Non-qualified withdrawals are subject to income tax and a 10 percent penalty.

UTMA/UGMA (UNIFORM TRANSFER/GIFT TO MINORS ACT)

These accounts aren't actually designed for education funding but can be used that way. An UTMA/UGMA is basically an account in a child's name that a custodian (usually a parent or grandparent) owns and manages. It depends on your state, but usually, the UGMA expires when the child reaches age eighteen, and the UTMA expires when the child turns twenty-one. This means when the child comes of age, they have full control of the account and can do whatever they want with it.

There is no tax-free growth in this type of account, but the funds are taxed at the child's tax rate and not the parent's, which can mean significant savings. The main benefit in accumulating funds in a UTMA/UGMA is the funds can be used for more than just college expenses.

GENERAL TAXABLE INVESTMENT ACCOUNT IN THE PARENTS' NAMES

This is just an investment account the parents set up and own in their own names that is earmarked for future education expenses. This way of saving does not have the tax benefits of the other account options listed above, but it does offer a great degree of flexibility. Since these funds are not in an education-specific account, they can be used for any expense that comes up, not just qualified education expenses. The parents are the owners, so if the funds are not needed for college, the parents can redirect the funds any way they please.

HOW MUCH TO SAVE

We all know college is expensive, but how much should you be saving now if you want to fund it for your kids? To fully fund four years of college for a baby born today, you will likely need to save somewhere between $400 and $600 a month until they are eighteen. There are a lot of factors involved in that calculation—where you live, the assumed rate of return on your investments, the assumed inflation (increase in price) of college tuition and general living expenses, etc.

How do most people fund it? They fund it through a combination of things. Generally, students have some form of scholarships or financial aid, the parents contribute some (pay as you go) or get loans, and some savings are applied.

As the parent, you should decide what you would like to target to pay for (if any) and start to save for that amount. Do you want to pay for four years of school? Two years? Nothing? Graduate school? Once you define that target, you can use an online calculator to figure out how much to save now to get there. The younger the child is, the more time the money has to compound and grow.

A common theme I see is people planning to save for one-third of college expenses. The idea is they will save for one-third of the costs, cash flow (pay as you go) for one-third, and the child will fund the remaining third with loans, working, or their savings. I think that is a great way to think about it.

Before I had kids, I saw many clients pay for college out of pocket. They hadn't saved a dime for college and would just pay the tuition bill as it came up. I was always floored by that. "How can someone afford an extra $20K a year to pay for college?" Now I know. When you have kids, a lot of your current income goes to them anyway. You are paying for their food, their clothing, their activities, and their care. When they go to college, you can just reallocate those funds toward their college expense needs. Anyone with kids in daycare is probably already paying tuition-like rates for that care, so it is already something that fits into your cash flow.

MAKE IT AUTOMATIC

Whatever you decide to do, make it automatic. If you decide you want to try to fund one-third through savings, then use an online calculator to see what that equates to now. Let's say it equates to $150 a month. Then, set up a 529 plan and have that amount automatically contributed from your bank account on the same day each month. Just pretend it is another bill to pay and make it automatic so you don't have to think about it.

You can also think of other ways to automate. Maybe you don't have the cash flow to meet your $150 target, so you're contributing twenty-five dollars a month. Then, you could say you will automatically contribute a percentage of any bonus or tax refund you receive to the 529 plan. If your kids get gifts of money from grandparents, you could automatically contribute all or a percentage of that to their 529 plan.

OTHER FUNDING OPTIONS

FAFSA (FREE APPLICATION FOR FEDERAL STUDENT AID)

By not filing their FAFSA, students miss out on nearly three billion dollars in Pell Grants each year, according to EducationData.org. You should plan to complete the FAFSA each year, even if you think you won't qualify for aid. It needs to be completed sooner than you think. You can fill it out as early as October 1st of the year *before* they will be attending college. Most colleges award some aid on a first come, first serve basis, so you don't want to miss out. The application must be received by June 30 of that year.

Dr. Ross Riskin, associate professor of Taxation and Certified College Financial Consultant, notes sometimes parents neglect to save for college, thinking that if they do, they will qualify for less financial aid. This is a common misconception. Riskin states that qualifying or not qualifying for aid is mostly income-based—not savings-based, so parents should not be afraid to save.

COLLEGE SCHOLARSHIP SERVICE (CSS) PROFILE

While the FAFSA checks your eligibility for federal funds, the CSS Profile determines eligibility for institutional awards and grants (aid given by the school itself). About four hundred schools are linked to the CSS, so if your child is going to one of them, you should fill this out too.

Here are some other scholarship websites to check out:
CareerOneStop.org
FastWeb.com
Scholarships.com

WHEN TO HAVE "THE TALK"

The college talk should be *way* easier than the other talk you have to have with your kids, but both should happen before they get to high school. Author Beth Kobliner says, "Talking about college is actually a series of mini-talks." She says you should plant seeds and have small conversations when they are eighth graders and young high schoolers so they are ready for a bigger conversation when they hit tenth through eleventh grade.

You should be ready to discuss what you have saved for and are willing to fund and what they will need to figure out a way to fund through savings, work, or loans, and how that impacts their future. They need to understand college is expensive and is a big decision that shouldn't be taken lightly. It is best to set these expectations early so they are not surprised when they can't go to an expensive liberal arts school in another state. Compare costs and values together. Also, talk about their career choice and what type of salary that equates to. Passion is one thing, but earning a living needs to be considered. If you and your partner are both attorneys making high incomes and your kids are used to a big house, new cars, and extravagant vacations, they could be disappointed if they cannot have that type of lifestyle in a lower-earning vocation.

EDUCATION ISN'T ONE-SIZE-FITS-ALL

When we think of post-high school education, we default to a four-year degree program. That isn't always necessary or the right fit for your child. Trade school programs are in high demand and typically take less than half the time and money to complete.

Since COVID-19 forced the world to figure out how to learn online, countless programs are available that provide students with degrees without them ever living on campus. Get creative with education and design a plan that works for your family. Don't just do what the neighbors are doing.

Being a lifetime learner is important, and those who specialize in something and continue to grow typically do better in their career or trade. Your kid's path may look different from yours, and that's okay.

"MONEY BOSS" SYSTEMS FOR SUCCESS—CHAPTER 8

- Start talking with your kids about college before they start high school.
- Use online calculators to determine your monthly savings targets.
- Make it automatic. If college savings are important to you, make it a "bill" that you pay each month on autopilot.
- Apply for the FAFSA in October the year *before* your student is attending college.

- Apply for scholarships and the FAFSA every year even if you think you don't qualify.

THE FUNNIES

EIGHT WAYS PARENTHOOD IS JUST LIKE COLLEGE

- You constantly feel hungover.
- You are occasionally vomited on by others.
- Mac 'n' cheese with microwave popcorn is a perfectly suitable meal choice.
- You must sometimes deal with unreasonable tantrums from people who are not currently capable of rational thinking.
- It is perfectly acceptable to leave the house in clothes you slept in the night before.
- The flawless chugging technique you developed to polish off the last drop of beer at closing time is now deployed daily to drain your coffee mug as you are sprinting out the door each morning.
- Pinterest-worthy crafting skills—you used to make home-made beer bongs with three dollars' worth of supplies from Ace Hardware. Now you make animal-shaped edible party favors out of organic popcorn for people who drink bath water regularly.
- You used to recite every word to Warren G's "Regulators" like a boss. Now you can do the same with that perky theme song from *Paw Patrol.*

CHAPTER 9

FOR THE LOVE—MONEY AND RELATIONSHIPS

———

It was 1996. I was in middle school, my dad was working as a lineman in a factory, and my mom worked the cash register at a liquor store. Middle school is the Super Bowl of awkwardness in one's life, particularly for girls. At the time, I was five foot seven and weighed about eighty pounds. I looked like a popsicle stick with a perm. I was all legs and ears, and the only curves to be seen were sitting on my nose—a pair of large, round, clear-rimmed glasses. I didn't have access to "tall" jeans, so my inseam was usually at least three inches shy of my sock line. There was no water for miles, but I was always ready for a flood in Salina, Kansas.

One of my mom's coworkers had three daughters who frequently gave us bags of hand-me-down clothing. Whenever that tub of clothes would arrive, it was better than Christmas! Everything was name brand—Z. Cavaricci jeans, Guess tops, and those cool Umbro shorts with the alternating checkerboard pattern on them. Jackpot! Where did they get all these amazing clothes?

I did not know what the term meant at the time, but my dad was frequently "on furlough" at the plant. I didn't sense anything was wrong. It was just cool he was at home after school every day. One day, I was wearing one of the super trendy tops that said GAP on it in *huge* letters (we didn't even have a Gap in our town, so this was pretty cutting edge). The original owner of the shirt made a comment as I passed by her locker: "Yeah, her dad lost his job again, so she wears my old clothes."

I was stunned. I felt embarrassed and exposed. It hadn't occurred to me I should be ashamed of wearing used clothing and that her family was somehow better than mine because her dad had a presumably "better" job. I never wore anything they gave us again to spare myself future public embarrassment.

As an adult, I still have a bit of a complex about clothing. I would not say I am on trend by any means (my college-age babysitters can confirm this), but I do make sure I have nice, quality clothing and outfits that make me feel confident and fit well. I make sure my kids have clothing that fit right and are semi-stylish. When we got married, this became a source of tension with my husband as he couldn't understand why I was always buying new clothes (especially when we lived in an eight-hundred-square-foot apartment that only had one closet).

When you ask my husband about his first memories of money, he'll say, "There never were any." He grew up on a farm and remembers having newborn calves in the house during the winter because they couldn't afford for them to die in the icy cold. Cattle was currency to their family, and if the cattle didn't survive, they didn't survive. He has vivid memories of his parents counting out change at the gas station to make sure they had enough to fill up the tank. He is terrified of being poor and never wants to feel the kind of financial stress his parents lived through.

START WITH UNDERSTANDING
YOUR PARTNER'S "WHY"

Money is such a complex topic and manifests differently in our experiences and memories. To some, money may symbolize freedom, power, and joy. Others may associate money with shame, greed, and sin. Many of our attitudes about money are set before we are even out of grade school and are further shaped by our life experiences along the way. Everyone has a past with money, so when people couple up in a marriage or partnership, there is often a disconnect in their views, and they must work together to find common ground.

As financial planners, we know emotions drive a lot of decisions around money. We need to understand where our clients are coming from and how they view money before we can do effective work for them. When we meet with a couple for the first time, we often have them complete an assessment about their "Fiscalosophy" (an assessment tool developed by

Mitch Anthony) or their attitudes about money. This gives us a backdrop to work from and often is an eye-opening conversation for the couple as they might not know these things about each other.

Laura Rotter, owner of True Abundance Advisors, says, "In my first meeting with a couple, I have them explore their individual money stories through a series of questions: what was your first experience earning money? Was money used in your family to reward? To control? What lessons about money did you learn from watching your mother? Your father?"

These are great questions to ask each other in a partnership. You may be surprised at what you find out. Understanding your partner's past experiences will help the two of you to grow together going forward.

"Being open, honest, and understanding each other's priorities when it comes to money is crucial to your overall financial health and success as a couple."
—JASON THACKER, HEAD OF CONSUMER
DEPOSITS AT TD BANK

WHEN TO TALK MONEY

People would rather talk about anything other than money. There is something so taboo about it. Sex, drugs, and even politics are less worrisome table topics than a disclosure of your salary or debt balances. This is why a lot of couples shy away from money conversations until it's too late.

"Forty-one percent of divorced Gen Xers and 29 percent of Boomers say they ended their marriage due to disagreements about money."

—TD AMERITRADE 2018

Millennial couples are more receptive to talking about their finances with their partner than previous generations. According to CNBC, 75 percent of millennial couples talk about money at least once a week, and it is making them happier. This is about 9 percent higher than Gen X couples and 31 percent higher than boomer couples. By having money discussions more often and being transparent, couples are addressing issues sooner, preventing mistakes, and not letting money problems grow and get out of hand. Roughly 80 percent of couples in all age groups who talk about money at least once a week report being happy in their relationships, TD Bank discovered.

"The 'Money Talk' is not a 'one and done.'"

—MANISHA THAKOR, FOUNDER OF MONEY
ZEN, AUTHOR OF GET FINANCIALLY NAKED:
HOW TO TALK MONEY WITH YOUR HONEY

As with anything of importance, you must make the time to have this talk. Talking about money weekly seems to be a good cadence for couples, so you could schedule thirty minutes a week after the kids go to bed or on a Sunday afternoon. It doesn't have to be a full, comprehensive review, just a discussion of upcoming expenses and what is going on in the next week. If you are paying off debts, this would be a good time to check your progress and scheduled payments. If you are saving up for something specific, like a vacation or remodel, you could check your savings balances and celebrate your progress. If weekly is too often, I'd suggest talking about money at least once a month or every pay cycle.

When you do sit down to chat, ideally you are not in a state of stress. When we are stressed, we lose the capability to make good decisions. Dr. Sonya Lutter, PhD, CFP®, professor and owner of Lutter Consulting, cited ways to identify if you are in a heightened state of physiological stress. When our bodies go into "fight or flight" mode, the blood rushes to our heart and other organs, so that can leave our extremities feeling cold. That is why in the case of a runaway bride, they say, "She got cold feet." When you are about to have an important conversation with your spouse, reach out and hold their hand for a minute. If it is cold, they might be in a state of stress, and you should navigate the conversation differently.

Find a safe space and time to talk about money and values. If you are trying to have a conversation while you're unloading the dishwasher and screaming at the kids to brush their teeth, it probably won't go anywhere. Don't accuse, don't be defensive, and remember you're in this together, and you both have a vested interest in a solution.

Come to the table with openness, empathy, and curiosity, not fear or blame. Remember, you are on the same team and are working together for the greater good. You are having these conversations so you can course correct if you're heading down the wrong path. Having these discussions early and often prevents them from becoming bigger issues that take more time and energy to fix. Manisha Thakor says if you are not having money conversations as a couple, "There are cracks in the foundation of your relationship. Cracks grow over time."

HOW HOUSEHOLD RESPONSIBILITIES
FACTOR INTO THE EQUATION

It is not uncommon for one spouse to be the dominant financial person in the house. This usually means they balance the checkbook (or reconcile the online tracking system), handle bill paying, and have a better sense of the overall financial health of the family than the other spouse does. There is nothing inherently wrong with that as long as the other spouse is privy to what is going on, has a baseline understanding of the situation, and agrees on the couple's common goals. When the other spouse is not well informed, this can cause friction or misunderstandings. For instance, they might use the wrong debit card or cause an account to overdraft if they don't understand how the financial system works.

If you are the one who manages the bulk of the household finances, you should ask your spouse if they are getting the information they would like to know. Ask them what questions they have or what changes they'd like to see made. You may find their interest has changed. Maybe they do want to know how much the mortgage is and when the daycare bill is paid.

Dr. Sonya Lutter, PhD, CFP®, professor and owner of Lutter Consulting, hosts a Love and Money curriculum where couples go through a series of exercises together over a six-week time frame. The purpose of the courses are not financial education; it is about communication and the emotional side of money. One of the exercises involves discussing household responsibilities. She has found in most cases, couples have spoken or unspoken rules about who does what in the relationship that develop early on. Over time, the couple evolves and changes, but that list of responsibilities does not.

Once children are brought into the equation, the household responsibilities increase and change significantly. Typically, the mother (whether she works outside the home or not) takes on most of the new responsibilities. A study by *The Atlantic* found married American mothers spend almost *twice* as much time on housework and childcare as do married fathers. Even though mothers today are far more likely to be working outside the home than in past decades, they spend *more* time on childcare than moms did in the 1960s.

Back in the *Mad Men* era, most women didn't work outside of the home and handled all the household responsibilities while the husband went out and earned money. There still seems to be a widespread belief that women should take on the bulk of the household duties, even if the husband is the one staying home with the kids. Dr. Lutter's research concluded women actually do *more* housework if they earn more money than their husbands. It's like they feel like they are required to bear more of the burden at home just because they are women.

FROM FUNCTIONING TO FLOURISHING

"Money is not just a tool to help us get through life and avoid catastrophe. Money helps us live life optimally so we don't just function but can flourish."

—DR. SARAH ASEBEDO, PHD, CFP®

It is so easy to live life in a passive state, simply reacting to events and issues as they come up and never feeling like you are completely in control. We can quickly get trapped in a cycle of just getting through the day or just getting to the next paycheck and not enjoying the present or giving any thought to the future. In my discussions with Dr. Martin Seay, PhD, CFP®, he talked about the concept of a "well-being budget." This is not a budget in the traditional sense. What he is referring to is being intentional with our money and our time—our two most valuable resources. When we align how we spend our money and how we spend our time with our values, only then can we truly live life "on purpose."

Traditional psychology focuses on treatment—helping people get from a sub-optimal place back to functioning or back to "normal." Positive psychology takes that a step further, so people are not just surviving but thriving. In their research on the work of positive psychologist Martin Seligman, Dr. Asebedo and Dr. Seay found that to get to a state of flourishing, one must be experiencing these five key elements in their life:

- Positive emotion
- Engagement
- Relationships

- Meaning
- Accomplishment

These five things manifest differently for everyone, but here are some examples of each.

Positive emotions can include gratitude, love, hope, joy, comfort, amusement, and pride. You can experience more of these emotions by doing activities you enjoy, spending time with people you love, and reminiscing about good times in your past.

Engagement happens when you are doing something you love and lose track of time. This is generally where our natural talents, strengths, and interests collide.

Relationships are key to having a fulfilling life. Humans naturally want to be around others who make them feel loved, safe, and supported.

Meaning is something people are always striving for. We want to feel like we have a purpose in life and are a part of something bigger than ourselves. We often find meaning in our vocations, religion, volunteer work, or creative endeavors.

Accomplishment as defined in Seligman's work is achievement, mastery, or competence. We feel accomplished when we reach our goals, master a new skill, or finish what we started.

Dr. Seay and Dr. Asebedo suggest doing something as simple as a daily gratitude exercise can help you zone in on identifying these five elements in your life. They recommend writing down or recounting three things that went well at the end of each day. This helps you remember the good things that occurred and your part in making them happen. During the height of the COVID-19 pandemic, my husband and I actually started doing this with our kids each night. That time was so hard on all of us. We were ripped from our routines and forced to figure out how to homeschool our kids while working and staying safe and sane at the same time. Yet we found little things we were thankful for each day, and we chose to focus on those instead of all the negative things we easily could have focused on. I learned I must actively choose to see the joy in each day and focus on what I can control. This is a practice we still continue today. It is so much fun to hear the things our children share about what they are thankful for.

This is one of many great graphics by Carl Richards of The Behavior Gap.

When you focus on things that are important to you and take control of their role in your life, you will feel more fulfilled and have better relationships with those around you. Take the time to study your history with money and some of the stories that have shaped who you are today. Keep looking for the bright spots and start living your life on purpose.

"MONEY BOSS" SYSTEMS FOR SUCCESS—CHAPTER 9

- Schedule time to talk money with your spouse/partner at least monthly or every pay cycle.
- Share your past money experiences that have shaped who you are today.
- Talk about who is responsible for household duties and re-evaluate every year as life changes.
- Start a gratitude practice and identify three things you are thankful for at the end of each day.

CHAPTER 10

PREPARING FOR THE FINANCIAL IMPACT OF MATERNITY LEAVE AND RETURNING TO WORK WITH EASE

———

"One minute you are fashionable and cool, and the next you are ordering one-piece bathing suits from L.L.Bean."

—JAMIE BOSSE, CFP®, RFC®

PREPARING FOR THE FINANCIAL IMPACT OF MATERNITY LEAVE

It does not matter if it's your first baby or your fifth, being pregnant is such an amazing, terrifying, and special time. Before you start packing up your desk and laptop, there are a few things you should know about maternity leave. In most cases, some or all your leave will actually be *unpaid*, leaving you with the options of using vacation time, taking less time off, or simply not being paid for the duration of your leave. Some companies require you use a portion of your vacation time, while others do not. If you have short-term disability insurance, you will likely receive a portion of your pay while you are on leave. However, most of these policies are pretty vague, and your Human Resources representative may not know the full details offhand. Here are three financial considerations when preparing for maternity leave—know your benefits, plan ahead for expenses, and understand the impact on your future income.

1. KNOW YOUR BENEFITS

If you have a disability policy, get familiar with the details. The policy language may be vague or confusing. It may say something to the effect of "60 percent of pay up to twelve weeks," leading you to believe you will receive 60 percent of pay for twelve weeks, when that is not the case. Prior to your due date, make sure you understand the full details. In my experience, a birth qualifies for 60 percent of pay for six to eight weeks (six weeks for a traditional birth, eight weeks for cesarean birth/additional complications). There is also a one to two week waiting period included in that time frame, meaning your actual pay period may only include four to six weeks. Sometimes this is paid out in a lump sum after the birth, and other times it will be paid out over several weeks.

If your employer pays the premiums for this disability policy, you will owe taxes on the funds you receive, so plan on withholding about 20 to 30 percent of what you receive for taxes. If *you* pay the premiums for the policy, you will not be taxed on the funds received. Additionally, you may need to reimburse your employer if they paid your portion of health insurance premiums (if the policy is through your employer) while you were on leave. Before your maternity leave, discuss the details with your manager to determine if you can continue to pay these premiums during your leave, or if they will need to be reimbursed upon your return. There is also typically a maximum amount you can receive per week, so if you are accustomed to a higher salary, this may be an additional reduction. After all these things are considered, you may only receive the equivalent of one to two net paychecks during that twelve-week period.

2. PLANNING AHEAD FOR EXPENSES

According to the USDA (2020), the cost of raising a child through age seventeen is $233,610 on average. *Yikes!* Luckily, all these expenses don't hit at once, but there are some big-ticket items you need to acquire before the baby is born, and there are significant changes to make to your spending plan going forward. First, make a list of the more expensive items you will need and the items you would like to have:

- Car seat (average price between fifty dollars and $300)
- Nursery Furniture—crib, dresser, changing table, rocking chair, etc.
- Stroller—might need adapters or attachments as well (average cost between fifty dollars and $300 for a traditional stroller. All-terrain or athletic high-end versions are usually in the $300 to $700 range).
- Highchair (average cost between seventy dollars and $150)
- Baby holding apparatuses—bouncy seat, swing, pack 'n play, wearable carrying devices, etc.

(Cost estimates acquired from CostHelper.com and CarSeatResearch.com)

Consider the timing of when you need these items and prioritize what you acquire first. For instance, you can't leave the hospital without a car seat, so that should be at the top of the list. I'd say a stroller is also a priority. Walks with the baby are a great sanity break while on maternity leave. Babies don't usually start eating food sitting up until they are around six months old, so the highchair purchase can be put off for a bit.

Now that you have a prioritized list of what you need, is there anything you can borrow from someone else? Check the selection at local consignment shops or Facebook Marketplace for gently used items. For the things you will need to purchase, split them up amongst the months you have remaining in your pregnancy, so you are not taking a large blow to your cash flow all at once. You will receive a lot of great gifts from friends and family members, but in my experience, these gifts tend to be blankets, adorable outfits, and toys—not the expensive items on your registry.

The things you spend money on each month are likely to change dramatically as well. Eating at nice restaurants, nights out with the guys or girls, and elaborate vacations may be replaced with diapers, daycare, and college fund contributions. The money you used to spend on nice purses, shoes, and clothing will now go to diaper bags, car seat accessories, and outfits for someone whose size changes monthly. You've made a plan for the big one-off items, and now you need to think about the regular additions to your monthly budget when your little nugget arrives. These include diapers, wipes, formula, baby food, etc. Diapers and formula are surprisingly expensive, and you go through them quickly, so be ready to purchase them often! You can investigate "subscribe and save" options on sites like Amazon Prime. These items will be delivered straight to your doorstep, saving you a trip to the store, and they usually give a discount for recurring orders.

A couple of weeks after the baby is born, bills may start rolling in from all directions. You should expect bills from the hospital, your doctor, the child's pediatrician, the anesthesiologist (if you received an epidural or required surgery), and any specialists who are needed. If you have a high-deductible health plan and have not met your deductible for the year, you may be paying full freight for these services until your deductible is met. If you have a health savings account (HSA), the good news is you may be able to use these funds to pay these bills. If you have a flexible spending account (FSA), you may be able to use these funds as well. Do not be afraid to ask your health providers about expected charges so that you can plan.

You will likely need to secure a daycare provider well in advance of the birth, which may require a financial deposit.

If your baby decides to make his or her debut earlier than scheduled or there are other complications, this may mean an extended hospital stay, requiring more unpaid time away from work. This is where the emergency fund we talked about in chapter two comes in handy.

3. UNDERSTAND THE IMPACT ON YOUR FUTURE INCOME

When you announced you were expecting, did your workflow change? Maybe you are not working on important projects or the most profitable cases anymore. If you are paid hourly, paid through commissions, have a heavy appointment schedule, or are expected to travel, your income may be impacted while you are pregnant or upon your return. Will you continue to work full-time after the baby is born? If not, what does your new role look like? Be sure to have an honest conversation with your employer about this. If they fear you will not return, you may not be considered for bonuses, an annual pay increase, or additional responsibilities. Communication is key. Be open and clear with your managers, coworkers, and clients about what you expect when you return to work and understand what is expected of you.

When you return to work, it is likely the clothes you used to wear will not fit. If you have a role where you need to dress professionally, you may need to invest in some new clothes. It seems to take at least nine to twenty-four months to return to "normal" size or to reach your "new normal" size after having a baby. Plus, if you are breastfeeding, you will want to wear clothes that allow for easy access to "the girls" so you do not have to completely disrobe at every pump break (i.e., no more side-zip dresses). Expect to need to go shopping and budget accordingly.

Taking a leave of absence from work can cause stress in your household if you are not prepared. Consider the issues above so you are not caught off guard by financial concerns. This way, you can spend your time worrying about your sweet little newborn instead of your finances.

GUIDE TO RETURNING TO WORK AFTER THE BABY

You blinked, and now your maternity leave is over. You are going back to work on Monday and feel totally unprepared. Instead of letting the dread and panic take over, get organized and make an action plan so you can take charge of this big transition. Here are six tips for making your return to work a little easier:

1. Establish protocol

What time do you need to leave the house? Who is doing daycare pickup and drop-off? What materials need to make it into the car each weekday morning? You have a good handle on how long it takes *you* to get ready in the morning, but how much time do you add to feed, dress, and prepare your little one for the day?

2. Practice pumping

If you plan to continue breast feeding after you return to the workplace, you and your breast pump will become very close!

Identify the times of day you'll need to take a pump break. (If the baby nurses every few hours, try to plan on 10:00 a.m., 1:00 p.m., and 4:00 p.m., or something of that nature.) Communicate that schedule to your coworkers by blocking thirty minutes on your calendar at those times each day to avoid scheduling issues. You'll probably only need fifteen minutes for the actual pumping, but you'll need to allow for some set up and clean up time. Get familiar with the territory. Where will you pump? Where is the sink to clean up? Where will you put your pump parts when they are wet? When I was pumping, I would rinse the pump parts and then steam clean them with microwave steam bags. This was always fun to explain in the break room:

Male coworker: "Is it lunch time already?"
Me (standing in front of the microwave at 10:30 a.m.): "Ha, ha! I am just steam cleaning the parts from the milk factory!"
Male coworker: "Huh?"
Me: "I am steam cleaning the parts to my breast pump."
Male coworker (turns red and looks at his feet): "Oh…cool. Well, see you later."

The steam clean only takes about one and a half minutes. No microwave? Bring one of those bottle brushes and clean them in the sink. I cleared out one of my desk drawers and lined it with towels to let the parts dry discreetly between pumping sessions. Will you store your milk in the fridge? I would put my bottle bag and ice brick in the freezer the night before, so it stayed nice and cold all day. I would just zip the bag closed tightly after I added each bottle, and it stayed cold until I could get it into my fridge at home.

3. Pack the night before

Mornings always seem to be hectic, especially when everyone needs to be somewhere at a certain time. Eliminate some of this chaos by laying out the baby's clothes and needed materials the night before and having a designated area in the fridge for what you need to grab on the way out. Select your outfit (shoes and jewelry included) the night before so you don't have to make a bunch of decisions during the crazy morning hours. Don't question your choice. Just put it on and get ready to go! You may want to have a backup outfit planned in the case of vomit, milk leaks, or explosive baby diarrhea. Once you have a child, you become a sort of mule. You may be carrying at least three bags (diaper bag, pumping bag, and purse) at all times, a car seat, as well as the actual infant, so you will literally have your hands full. The more you can have packed and ready to go the night before, the faster you will be able to get out the door.

4. Get up first and dressed last

I find if I am the first one awake in the house, I can usually get at least partially ready before someone else needs me. This *sucks* because you are exhausted and getting eight hours of blissful sleep is all you wish for, but it will make your morning easier if there is somewhere you need to be at a certain time. The bogey here is children wake up at all hours, so you can't always win at this! Have a plan for what you'll do with the baby if they are up, but you still need to get ready. It is good to have a playpen, bouncy seat, or highchair available to keep them safe and in sight while you attempt to conceal the bags under your eyes with a few layers of Mary Kay. It is also a good idea to not be fully dressed when handling an infant. In the mornings, their diapers are full and potentially overflowing, and they are liable to puke on you at any moment, especially if they are nursing in your lap. Wear a robe, full-coverage apron, or hazmat suit to protect your clothes from the unexpected. Even if you avoid any major catastrophes, you will likely find a cheerio or booger stuck to your shoulder as you enter your first meeting for the day.

5. Shower the night before to save time

I've always preferred showering in the mornings, but sometimes you just need to get creative (or skip the shower altogether). Washing my hair is no longer a priority. On days I must wash my hair (and dry it and style it), that takes up precious time in the morning that just isn't worth it. If my hair grease can be concealed by dry shampoo, I will delay the washing as long as possible. Don't judge me (or sniff my hair when you give me a hug). On days when my husband is out of town and I know we'll be in a rush in the morning, I shower the night before to shave some time off our morning schedule.

6. Enlist help and communicate

Moms are terrible at asking for help even when they really need it. I know you can handle it all, Mama, but cut yourself some slack occasionally! Vocalize what you are struggling with and let someone help you! Have a neighbor who walks by every morning and would love to cuddle your baby while you pack the car? Let her. Have a mother who will drop off the kids at daycare for you on Tuesdays? Let her. Your childless coworker always says, "Call me if you need me," so call her when you are stressed at 6:00 p.m., covered in puke, and trying to cook dinner. Let her hold the baby while you clean up and eat.

The biggest thing of all is communicating with your partner on how they can help. If you say, "I got this," they will believe you, and you will just continue to be in a constant state of stress. Give them specific instructions so they know when they are supposed to cook dinner, do daycare pickup, or pack the diaper bag. Simply ask them to fold the laundry once a week or hold the baby so you can shower in peace. Dads can't read your mind even though we think they should be picking up on our obvious signals. Your partner doesn't know what is on that huge to-do list in your head, so communicate what you need help with and let them help you! Also, your coworkers may not understand why you must pump over lunch instead of going to the local burger joint or why you can't be in six back-to-back meetings during the day. Be sure you communicate your new schedule and how you are working around it.

Getting into your new work routine after being on maternity leave is tough. It is an emotionally and physically challenging time, but by planning ahead and doing the items on this list, you will save yourself some time, stress, and headaches. Most importantly, go easy on yourself! Adjusting to parenthood and all the juggling that comes with it is exhausting and will take some time. Being a mom is the most rewarding *and* most thankless job in the world. It is amazing and exhausting. Hang in there!

"MONEY BOSS" SYSTEMS FOR SUCCESS
SUMMARY—CHAPTER 10

- Know your maternity leave benefits.
- Plan ahead for new purchases you will need to make for the baby.
- Understand the impact maternity leave will have on your future income.
- Communicate and ask for help when you need it.

CHAPTER 11

TEACHING KIDS ABOUT MONEY WHEN IT IS INVISIBLE

"Money is central, but it is also a teaching tool that uses the value of a dollar to instill in our children the values we want them to embrace. These traits—curiosity, patience, thrift, modesty, generosity, perseverance, and perspective."

—RON LIEBER, THE OPPOSITE OF SPOILED

Picture this: it is one of those random Monday holidays when school is closed. I have my kindergartener, Oscar, with me for the day. It is cold and rainy, so we head to Target for something to do and to knock out my shopping list before the rest of the offspring are released from daycare. In true five-year-old fashion, Oscar would like to own every third item he lays eyes on. Here's a pro tip: if you are shopping with anyone under the age of twelve, avoid the toy section altogether. His desires are fleeting. Initially, he just *had* to have the light up Thanos glove with the removeable infinity stones. Then, he moved onto a pack of Pokémon cards. He lets out an audible gasp when he sees it—a fifty-nine-dollar remote control Grave Digger monster truck.

Oscar: "Mom, can we please buy this?"
Me: "Nope, that is not in our spending plan for today."
Oscar: "Well, why don't you just buy it on Amazon then?"

Oscar doesn't realize buying things on Amazon actually costs money. This concept just doesn't make sense to him. Things at the store cost money because we must pay for them before we leave, but Amazon is different. In his eyes, it is a magical service that lives in Mom's phone and will deliver whatever your heart desires right to your front door.

FINANCIAL EDUCATION IS NOT TAUGHT IN SCHOOL

In the introduction of this book, I shared that my parents filed for bankruptcy when I was in college. I would like to tell you my parents' misfortune was a result of something out of their control—an expensive health issue, an accident, or a business deal gone south. That's not the case. They were just regular middle-class Americans who got caught up in a crazy debt cycle with credit cards. I'd also like to tell you they are an anomaly, and most people don't get themselves into these situations, but sadly, that's not the case either.

We don't have to look very far for news about how financially troubled our society is. You've seen the headlines—"Every Year Over 700,000 Americans File for Bankruptcy" (*Ascent* 2020), and "78 Percent of Workers Live Paycheck To Paycheck" (*Forbes* 2019), student loan debt is at all-time highs, etc. It's not just the lower classes that are struggling. Even folks with great careers and six-figure incomes have trouble managing a monthly budget and being prepared for emergencies. How did we get here?

Well, for starters, we were never taught about financial education in school. So, what we did learn we picked up from our parents or friends, and the rest was trial and error. For kids today, that same dynamic exists, but it is even harder to navigate because money has become almost completely intangible. When I was a kid, I either had cash in my pocket or I didn't, and that determined whether I could buy something. As I got older, I had a physical checkbook to manage so I was aware of my balances and where my money went.

I find young kids today really have no concept of money or how it works. All they see is their mom and dad swiping a card at Target or pushing a button on their phone, and Amazon boxes full of stuff just magically appear on their doorstep. How do we teach kids about money when it is invisible? It is now more important than ever to be very intentional when we are talking about money and teaching these lessons and habits to our kids. We must look for teachable moments and create them where we can.

Kids are sponges eager to soak up information. They want to know about money mainly because money can lead to new stuff (they love stuff!), so use their curiosity to your advantage. In previous generations, the topic of money has been pretty taboo. It wasn't long ago husbands didn't even tell their wives how much money they made, much less discuss it with children. If your kids are asking questions about money, don't shy away from the conversation or make it seem like they shouldn't talk about it. We *want* money to be a normal topic of conversation. You want them to keep coming to you with questions about money (and other things in life), so it is important you address their questions, be honest, and have a conversation about it. If you make it awkward, they will likely stop coming to you with questions and will get their information from other sources—like kids on the playground or the internet, and you don't want either of those to be their go-to place for information.

It is also important to be aware of gender stereotypes. A study Ron Lieber cited in the *Opposite of Spoiled* noted we still gravitate toward having money conversations with our sons and not our daughters. It is so important not to foster these stereotypes in your home. Financial topics should be addressed with *all* kids. In 2019, I was looking into this app you can use to manage allowances. In conversations with the developer, they estimated 50 percent of the time parents are paying their daughters less for the same number of chores their sons are doing. The wage gap is real, folks.

In this chapter, we are going to discuss the financial concepts kids can grasp in each age group and ways to create teachable moments. The age groups and concepts defined here are from the Money as You Grow website.

FINANCIAL CONCEPTS TO LEARN
IN EACH AGE GROUP

"Good habits formed in youth make all the difference."

—ARISTOTLE

START 'EM YOUNG—FINANCIAL CONCEPTS TO
UNDERSTAND AT AGES THREE TO FIVE

I know this seems really young to be talking about money, but I can tell you from experience, kids this age are very interested in money and want to know more about it. In this age group, some of the concepts you can discuss include the following:

- **You need money to buy things.** Kids in this age group can understand the basic concept of commerce and exchanging money for goods or services. You can talk to them about the different forms of money we use—coins, dollar bills, and credit and debit cards. A good place to start is with more tangible forms of money, like identifying coins and their value. Start to talk about all the things that cost money—toys, groceries, their kids' meal at Chick-fil-A, etc. Also explain that a lot of things that have value are free. Spending time playing with a friend or cousin is really fun and doesn't cost a dime.
- **Money is earned by working.** Begin by explaining some people work for others and some start their own businesses. Talk about your job or profession and why you chose it. Use examples of jobs they recognize, like teachers, fire fighters, and mail carriers. Maybe you work from

home or work strange hours. Take some time to explain to them what you do while you're working so they understand why you are at the computer all day or gone for long periods of time. You can talk with them about ways they might think of to make money.

- **Sometimes you must wait before you can buy things you want.** Delayed gratification is a hard concept for a lot of adults to understand. The sooner your child accepts this fact, the better! Have them identify an item they'd like to buy. Maybe it is a toy or piece of candy. Talk about how much it costs and help them count out the money required to purchase it.

- **There is a difference between what you want and what you need.** Talk about all the things we need to buy with our money—clothing, food, and a home to live in. Then make a list of things we like to have, but don't necessarily need to live—more toys, candy, and *Paw Patrol* slippers.

FINANCIAL CONCEPTS TO UNDERSTAND AT AGES SIX TO THIRTEEN

Things get a lot more interesting at these ages as they tend to want more "stuff" and want to do more activities, so they need to understand the following concepts in addition to the concepts for three- to five-year-olds.

- **You must make a lot of choices when it comes to how you spend your money.** When you are at the store, you can talk about why you chose to purchase one item over another or give them the power to choose. Give them some money with the task of choosing which snacks to buy for the week. Do you want to spend money on something, or can you borrow it or buy it somewhere used or at a lower cost?

- **It is a good idea to compare prices and shop around before you decide to make a purchase.** Explain there are lots of ways to buy things. You can physically go into a store to buy it, look for it online (perhaps via the magical land of Amazon), or buy it used from someone else. They can help you look through coupons or wait for sales to get better pricing.

- **The concept of saving can be introduced in this age group.** You can talk about saving at least a dime for every dollar they earn and how interest works when you put money into a bank account. You can show some examples of compound interest and what they might gain if they forego a purchase today and save the money instead.

- **Using a credit card is really like a loan.** Most likely, they watch you use cards all the time and might have questions about it. They need to understand that when you use a card, a financial transaction is taking place and money is going out.

FINANCIAL CONCEPTS TO UNDERSTAND AT AGES FOURTEEN TO EIGHTEEN

This is where you start training them to be miniature adults and set them up for success in the working world.

- **You need to be having conversations about college.** Talk about what you have saved for/are willing to fund, what they will need to figure out a way to fund through savings, work, or loans, and how that impacts their future. It's best to set these expectations early so they are not surprised when they can't go to an expensive liberal arts school in another state. Compare costs and values together. Also, talk about their career choice and what type of salary that equates to. Passion is one thing, but earning a living needs to be considered. If you and your partner are both attorneys making high incomes and your kids are used to a big house, new cars, and extravagant vacations, they could be disappointed if they can't have that type of lifestyle in a lower-earning vocation.

- **Credit cards can be a tool, or they can be very dangerous.** They should understand that if you use a card, you need to be able to pay it off each month. Continue to talk about healthy credit card behaviors and how it is really like a loan. They need to understand if you don't pay the bill in full every month, interest can work against you, and you'll end up paying more for the item than it actually costs. At this age, they are close to having their own credit card.

- **The concept of taxes.** They may start doing part-time jobs at this point and need to understand their first paycheck will be much lower than they think due to taxes. This is an important concept to understand well before they graduate from college and get their first full-time job. Explain what taxes pay for in your community.

- **Basic investment concepts.** If they are earning income, you may consider setting up a Roth IRA (IRA stands for Individual Retirement Account) for them and talking about basic investment concepts so they can get some hands-on experience in watching their money grow.

FINANCIAL CONCEPTS TO UNDERSTAND
AT AGES EIGHTEEN AND OLDER

The goal by now is for the young adult to have a lot more autonomy and be ready to navigate the "real world" without a ton of help from parents.

- **Only use a credit card if you can pay it off in full each month.** The credit card discussions are super important now because they may have one and can get one without you knowing about it. I actually have a personal story about this. When I was a freshman in college, I signed up for my first credit card because they were giving away free t-shirts in front of the student union. A free t-shirt is not a good reason to sign up for a credit card. Then, I signed up for two more at a fundraiser where a friend was raising money for his fraternity trip—also a terrible reason to get a credit card. So, there I was, eighteen years old with three credit cards I was not ready for. You want your kids to be ready to navigate those situations better than I did.

- **Insurance is a concept they should understand.** Insurance is a form of managing risk and sharing costs. We pay to insure our home so if it burns down in a fire, the insurance will help pay for our next home. Talk about insurance on their car, how much it costs, and why it is important to have if they get in an accident. Renters' insurance is also a good idea. By now, they are likely getting ready to move out on their own or will soon. Explain that they have items of value in their rental home or apartment—their bed, their clothing, etc. If the fire scenario happens to their rental home, explain that if they pay a small amount of renters' insurance each month, the insurance will reimburse them for the lost or damaged items. Health insurance is also important. You pay a premium each month to share costs of doctor's appointments and treatments.

- **The concept of an emergency fund.** Hopefully, they've been in the habit of saving some of their earnings by this point. Provide examples of why it is important to keep at least three months' worth of expenses in savings at all times. You can cite examples of emergencies you've experienced—car accidents, refrigerators going out, losing a job, or medical issues—and how having a savings cushion helped you get through these times. Alternatively, talk about how you regretted not having an emergency fund when you needed it.

THE ALLOWANCE DEBATE

So, we know what they can understand at each age, but how do we create the teachable moments and start cementing good financial habits early on? Every resource I've seen on this topic shares the theme of teaching kids to work. One hundred years ago, once a kid was old enough to obey commands, they were working on the farm or in factories and had responsibilities around the house. Today the pendulum has swung pretty far in the other direction. Kids are busy with a ton of activities and feel like the world revolves around them. The terms "helicopter parent" and "lawnmower parent" are prevalent as parents are trying to protect their kids but end up setting them up for failure. These kids grow up to be enabled, unhappy, and incapable of facing a challenge or conflict on their own. In *The Opposite of Spoiled*, Ron Lieber states four factors that definitely spoil kids. Two of them include having no chores, tasks, or responsibilities to other people, and another is having no rules to follow or guidelines and schedules to stick to. Figuring out how to incorporate work into their lives squashes both of those factors. Plus, working is a life skill they are going to need to be successful adults. Work is just a part of life, and if you're not good at it, you will suffer.

I have read tons of books and articles on the topic of teaching kids about money. The subject that seems to be the most controversial is how to format the payments for said work. The allowance debate is a vexing discussion, and the outcome varies quite a bit from person to person. All agree you have to incorporate pay into their lives so they start learning about money. The problem is tying the compensation to chores or not. Most agree some chores are done as a part of living in the household and should not be rewarded or tied to pay. These chores may include putting their dirty clothes in the laundry, putting dishes in the sink after meals, making their bed, and other daily tasks. Some say "extra" chores on top of what is normally expected can be paid, and some say an allowance shouldn't be tied to work at all; it should just be the learning tool for managing money. In the book *Smart Money, Smart Kids*, Dave Ramsey says he hates the word allowance. He says that sounds like welfare, so he taught his kids to work on "commission." I can see both sides of the argument. I personally like the idea of tying the pay to work in some capacity since that is how you and I earn money and is how they'll earn money as adults. You can decide what is right for your family, but make sure you start to incorporate pay into their lives to make the lesson tangible.

Most kids can't go out and get a job at age five, so if you want them to experience work, you will have to create the work opportunity for them. So, how do you structure these working/learning opportunities? Again, it varies widely by age.

CREATING TEACHABLE MOMENTS—AGES THREE TO FIVE

This age group has an incredibly short attention span, so any chore they do must be short and simple. It is recommended to limit chores to two to three easy-to-remember tasks. You can pay fifty center to one dollar for every year of their age, pay one dollar per task, or set up some other way to manage it. Just remember, you need to be ready for payday at all times, so have bills or coins on hand. Three- to five-year-olds need immediate compensation to make the lesson stick. You must pay immediately upon completion and make it really exciting! Pump them up by telling them how big they are and that only big kids get the responsibility of doing chores.

POSSIBLE CHORES FOR THREE- TO FIVE-YEAR-OLDS

- Picking up toys
- Matching socks
- Feeding animals
- Collecting indoor trash cans for trash day

- Swiffering the floor (My kids love this one so much that I actually have two Swiffer sticks to avoid altercations over who gets to use it.)
- Putting their dirty clothes in the laundry
- Setting the dinner table (with supervision, of course)
- Carrying in groceries
- Making their beds

The focus for three- to five-year-olds is just to get in the mind-set of working, seeing a job through to the end, and being proud of a job well done. This age group is very visual, so putting their earnings in a clear container is a good way to build excitement around it. At our house, we initially started with traditional piggy banks and found the kids wanted to dump it out all the time to make sure the money was still in there, so now we use clear containers.

Saving money is a little hard to grasp at this point, so the main goal is *spending* money. You want them to decide on how to spend their money and take some responsibility for it, so they start to understand what things actually cost. Take them shopping to spend their earnings and make it fun.

CREATING TEACHABLE MOMENTS—AGES SIX TO THIRTEEN

At this age, kids want to do more things and buy more stuff, so their pay and responsibilities should increase. Now you can start paying weekly instead of immediately. This helps instill the concept of delayed gratification and patience. You will want to have a way to track the work that was done to be sure they get paid for it. This is where the chore chart on the fridge is helpful. If they do three of their chores instead of all five, then they only get three dollars instead of five dollars (or whatever your rate is).

POSSIBLE CHORES FOR SIX- TO THIRTEEN-YEAR-OLDS

- Anything from the three- to five-year-olds category
- Vacuuming
- Making *your* bed—this is something Jolene Godfrey suggested in *Raising Financially Fit Kids*. If making their own bed was just a part of being in the household and not a paid chore, they could be paid for making your bed or the guest room bed as a task.
- Yard work—like pulling weeds and raking leaves
- Dog walking
- Cleaning windows
- Folding laundry
- Babysitting (if properly trained)
- Unloading the dishwasher
- Watering plants
- Cleaning the car
- Preparing snacks
- Dusting furniture or baseboards

At this age, you can introduce the concept of saving as well as giving. Now, they can split up their income between what they will give, what they will save, and what they will spend. It is recommended to label separate containers or jars for giving, saving, and spending so they can make the process tangible. If giving is an important value you want to instill in your child, this is a good method for making it a habit. If not, you could choose to skip that jar. Some use jars, and others use envelopes or Tupperware containers, but whatever you do, you want to make sure it's exciting. Let your child know they are graduating to something big and encourage them to decorate the envelopes or jars as they wish.

At this age, spending is the main concept they already understand, and you're introducing more. The savings jar is basically just a long-term spending bucket. They are not trying to save up for college or a house, but it is good for them to start setting targets for things they'd like to save up for—most likely a toy or gadget of some kind that costs more than their weekly paycheck and something that takes a few weeks or a month to build up to. This teaches them goal-setting and delayed gratification and tests if they really do want the toy after waiting for it. Have you heard of the concept of waiting twenty-four hours when want to buy something to see if you actually still want to purchase it after you've cooled off a bit? You're teaching them that same concept here by letting them understand, "I want this item, but I don't have enough money for it, so I'll have to wait." You may find they forget all about the item once it's no longer in sight.

This reminds me of the concept of layaway. As an elder millennial, I participated in ancient customs such as this one. For younger millennials and Gen Zers, let me explain. Before everyone had credit cards, most stores offered layaway. You want to buy an item, but can't afford it today, so you would make a deposit on the item and the store would hold it for you for a period until you could "pay it off" and buy it outright. Kind of hilarious in today's world, huh? I was a habitual "layawayer" in high school. I would head to the Buckle, try on some cute tops I couldn't afford, and put them on layaway. Then, *if* I came back for them at all, I'd come back two weeks later and would have totally forgotten what the items were.

This is also the time when you let them start giving their own money to church or charity. It's different when they are giving away *your* money, but when it's theirs, it takes on a whole new perspective. Talk to them about what causes are important to them and where they might donate their money. Maybe it's the local pet shelter, the library, or the little red Salvation Army bucket around the holidays. If you typically give money every Sunday at church, let them put some of their hard-earned dollars in the offering plate as well.

The spend jar is fair game for them to spend on what they wish. You can still put some rules on dangerous items you won't allow them to purchase, but you want them to make some silly purchases and learn from them. The idea here is they need to practice and fail in order to learn. This generally goes one of two ways. Scenario one—they buy the toy, play with it for a week, and then it goes in the Goodwill pile. In this case, you can use this as an example of what *not* to do with future purchases. Scenario two—it turns out to be a great purchase. They get a ton of enjoyment and use out of it, and they are proud of themselves for making the commitment to save for it. This reinforces that saving is worth it.

If you are going on vacation, you can let them take some of their own spending money to buy souvenirs or candy you won't purchase for them. Rachel Cruze, financial guru and co-author of *Smart Money Smart Kids*, gives an example of how when she was this age, her family went to an amusement park, and she could take as much money as she wanted from her spending envelope to use on games. She spent all her money within the first ten minutes and begged her parents to give her more. They stuck to their guns and taught her the lesson that when it's gone, it's gone. She says she still remembers that lesson today. We want kids to experience "pain" and make mistakes when the stakes are lower. Sure, Rachel was sad and uncomfortable that day, but she learned a valuable life lesson in a safe environment. If she had not learned this lesson as a kid, as an adult, she may have had more issues with more serious consequences.

LET KIDS FAIL

As parents, we must step out of our helicopters and let kids fail. By letting them fail, they learn to get back up and try again instead of giving up and whining for help. If we are always bailing them out by running their homework to school for them and finishing their science projects, we are not doing them any favors. It's the same with financial concepts: we have to let them practice, fail, and learn how the real world works. It is better for them to fail now, as kids, when the stakes are lower.

"Your habits will determine your future."

—JACK CANFIELD

Now, let's move on to the older kids.

CREATING TEACHABLE MOMENTS—AGE FOURTEEN TO COLLEGE-AGE

At these ages, kids want a lot of specific stuff, like the coolest shoes, phones, and jeans, and they want to do a lot of activities with their friends. Now is the time to move to a checking account instead of a cash payday. You can take the amount you would normally spend on them for entertainment, clothing, and other needs and put that into their checking account each month and let them manage it. If they spend it all on a pair of designer sneakers in the first week and have no money to go to movies with friends later, they hopefully have learned money is finite, and they need to manage it better. At this age, if they feel they need more money, encourage them to be industrious and go out and make more. They can babysit, dog walk, or get a real part-time job to supplement their income. This can teach them that if they want more, they need to figure out how to do it themselves instead of relying on their mom and dad. This is a great quality to instill.

Working for someone other than their parents can be a really good thing. I know with all the travel sports teams and other obligations in which our kids participate, it can be hard to find time for part-time work. It doesn't have to be much, maybe just five to ten hours a week to give them a feel for the working world. They will learn customer service, that you must be on time and dependable for work, how to get along with others, and how to work with a manager. This is also good training for filling out tax forms and learning firsthand that your paycheck isn't as big as you think it's going to be. You want them to learn this while they are still under your roof.

When they are ready to leave the nest, you want them to have some work experience and understand they can't have everything they want right when they want it. You want them to be comfortable handling money and know how to think ahead to make their paycheck last.

GETTING ADULT KIDS OFF THE PAYROLL

What about the "kids" who aren't really kids anymore? You might be thinking, "Man, this is good information, but it's twenty-five years too late!" I've seen clients who are still giving their thirty-two-year-old kids an allowance and paying their cell phone and car insurance every month. A study by *Forbes* concluded 59 percent of parents provide financial support to their adult children who are no longer in school—sometimes continuing well into their forties. The levels of support vary from simply allowing the young adult to live in their house (or a house they own) rent-free to paying their bills, buying their cars, and even buying their groceries. This is really tough for parents. We all want the best for our children, and we want them to have a "better life than we did." Most of all, we hate to see them struggle or suffer, so we swoop in to help however we can. The important point to get across is we are not helping our kids by doing this. We are actually inhibiting them from becoming productive, independent adults.

In some cases, supporting adult kids financially is absolutely necessary, such as during times of crisis, like the COVID-19 pandemic, when people are suffering, and jobs are hard to come by. Maybe they are going through a divorce and need help in the short term until they are back on their feet. Maybe they suffer from a mental illness that inhibits their ability to earn income or live independently. It is absolutely fine to help adult kids in these instances. It's even fine to bail out adult kids who aren't suffering from time to time—just make sure they are learning a lesson each time instead of taking advantage of you. If they make $30,000 a year, they need to learn to live like someone who makes $30,000 a year.

Most often, the adult child has been sheltered or enabled for most of their life. They've never had to pay a bill before, don't know how much their cell phone costs, and charges daily expenses on a credit card someone else pays off every month. They may not even fully understand the financial concepts we talked about for six- to thirteen-year-olds and have never learned what life actually costs. If you are in this spot, start with the basics. Help the adult child understand what their expenses are, even the ones you pay. Sit down and list out all their inflows and outflows. Figure out the fixed bills for which they need to be prepared each month and then what's left for groceries, gas, and entertainment. You don't have to stop cold turkey. Set some time frames and slowly decrease your monthly stipend until they are off the payroll completely. You must start making things uncomfortable to motivate them to take responsibility to make money themselves or figure out how to manage the money they have in a better manner. This could be stretched out over six, twelve, or maybe eighteen months depending on the circumstances. You don't want to make their lives so easy they want to live with you forever. If you can teach them to live within their means, that is a skill that will benefit them for a lifetime.

When reporters asked famous actor Jackie Chan why he has chosen to give all his wealth to charity instead of passing it on to his only son, I think they were expecting a great news story—a juicy family controversy, family secrets revealed, etc. Instead, Jackie simply said, "If he is capable, he can make his own money. If he's not, then he will just be wasting mine."

I think his message there is we are doing the best for our kids by empowering them to be independent and stand on their own two feet and giving them the tools to build a great life for themselves.

When I was a sophomore in college, I had three credit cards, and my parents had filed for bankruptcy. If I wasn't careful with the steps I took in my life, my story could have played out just as theirs did. Instead, I decided to recognize my shortcomings and arm myself with knowledge. After hearing news of the bankruptcy, I decided to take a personal finance class so I could learn how to better handle my money and learn the skills necessary for a healthy financial life. My story has a happier ending because I empowered myself with education. No matter what age your kids are, it's not too late to start learning.

Like with most things, the sooner you start, the better. If you can ingrain a behavior early on, the better it will stick. Kids who grow up with a good education around money and healthy habits will grow into adults who are less likely to get stuck in a dangerous debt cycle, are better prepared for emergencies, and have surplus to give to charity and support their communities.

"MONEY BOSS" SYSTEMS FOR SUCCESS SUMMARY—CHAPTER 11

- Talk to your kids about money early and often.
- Create teachable moments through work and pay.
- Let kids fail while the stakes are lower.

CONCLUSION

———

*"Life is what happens when you are
busy making other plans."*

—JOHN LENNON

Congratulations for getting this far on your journey to
becoming a money boss! I hope you learned a few things
and feel more confident in your money management skills
than you did when you first picked up this book. Life is too
short to be continuously overwhelmed and consumed by
financially induced stress.

So, what now? We covered a ton of topics in this book, and
that can sometimes cause information overload. Don't fret;
here's an action plan to break down next steps to apply what
you've learned.

Do ONE thing.

That's it. Just commit to doing one thing differently than you were before to improve your financial life for the better. Commit to doing one new thing each month for the next six months. Once you establish the habit and get the system in place, it generally doesn't require much maintenance going forward. Every month is a fresh start to add a new system. Here are some ideas based on the "Money Boss Systems for Success Summaries" at the end of each chapter:

Month 1—Find Your WHY—Chapter References 1 and 9

- Take the Money Script Assessment to gain insight on why you make the decisions you do around money.
- Create the vision you want for your life. Who do you want to be?
- Make time for money conversations with your spouse or partner.

Month 2—Build the Foundation—Chapter Reference 2

- Start building your emergency fund.
- Automate your saving and investing so you don't have to think about it.

Month 3—Get Control of Cash Flow—Chapter Reference 3

- Align your money with your values.
- Automate most bills and savings.
- Be sure to account for non-monthly expenses, like Christmas, summer camp, and car maintenance, in your monthly spending plan.

Month 4—Risk Management—Chapter References 4 and 5

- Make sure you have at least seven to ten times your income in life insurance coverage (probably a twenty- to thirty-year term life insurance policy).
- Get a basic estate plan in place—a will, power of attorney for healthcare, general power of attorney, and advanced directive.

Month 5—The Long-Term Game—Chapter References 6, 7, and 8

- Take advantage of your company retirement plan. Contribute at least up to the match and increase your contribution by 1 percent every year (or as you get pay increases) until you get up to 15 percent.
- Focus on "boring" investments for your money.
- Take advantage of tax-free growth in 529 plans for college savings (only after you have your retirement savings going).

Month 6—Improving Future Generations—Chapter Reference 11

- Talk to your kids about money.
- Find a way to pay them so they can start learning basic money principles before they leave the nest.

Be patient with yourself. Changing habits and behaviors takes time and effort. This is not something that happens overnight. Just tackle one thing at a time knowing all those things will start to add up and pay off in the long run. When you implement a new system or check something off your list, celebrate your success! Every change you make gets you closer to the life you want to be living. Your future self will thank you! Take control of your money so you can shift your focus to the things and people who matter most.

ACKNOWLEDGMENTS

———

So, writing the acknowledgments page might just be the hardest part of writing a book. This book has been in my head and in the works for *years*, and you wouldn't be reading it today without the help and encouragement of so many wonderful people along the way.

I definitely couldn't have done it without the love (sometimes "tough" love) and support of my amazing husband, Weylan. You've been my number one fan throughout this long and crazy process and, most importantly, you helped me hide from the kids when I had deadlines to meet. I can't believe we finally did it!

To Grandma Paula (Mom) and Grandpa Jim Jim (Dad), thank you *so much* for taking the kids for a few days and weekends during the final push. I really appreciate you!

Ellie, Auggie, Oscar, and Landry, I know it's been hard this past year while I've been locked away in my office missing out on your playtime and snuggles. I hope you are proud of the things I create and know I love you to the moon and back.

Sarah Baker, I wouldn't have made it through the editing process without the jazzy rap songs you sent over to keep me going. Thank you for always trying to cheer me up, even during my lowest moments.

To KPat and Colleen, thank you for always believing I would be "famous" one day. I never made it on *The Ellen DeGeneres Show*, but we'll see if Kelly Ripa can squeeze me in sometime!

To my "Heavy Pen" readers—Wendy Johnson, Mikayla Stover, Christyn Zins, Kim Bridges, Debbie Glick, Patrick Frank, and Pam Miller—you guys are TheBomb.com! I am so grateful you took time to comb through several chapters and offer your reviews and feedback. This was key to making the book what it is today.

Thank you, thank you, *thank you* to everyone who took time out of their busy schedules to be interviewed for this book. Amy Mullen, Sonya Lutter, Martin Seay, Sarah Asebedo, Travis Tannahill, Summer Ott Dierks, Nick Raich, Dawn Crouch, Laura Rotter, Ross Riskin, and Hannah Moore— your wisdom and expertise brought this book to a whole other level.

Thank you to TJ for saying he will only read my book in audio format. I initially wasn't thinking about making this an audiobook, but the world needs to hear this Mickey Mouse voiceover.

The humblest of thanks to everyone who purchased a copy of my book in the pre-sale and helped me post about it and advertise it. You guys made the financial hurdles of publishing a book so much more manageable.

Aaron and Joni Plante	Abbie Rondeau-Nelson
Abby Moore	Adryanna Drake
Allan Naranjo	Allie and Steve Lampe
Allison Disbrow	Amanda Hoeppner
Angela Kreps	Ann Walter
Anna Tomei	April Jacobs
Asha Aravidakshan	Ashley Graff
Aspyre Wealth Partners	Begona Pino
Benjamin Lloyd	Bret and Laura Henderson
Bridget Butkievich Martin	Brittney and Layne Lohmeier
Brooke and Matt Mingenback	Chris and Amy Payne
Christianna Peterson	Christin and Tyler Billinger
Christyn and Tony Zins	Colleen Wysong
Cortnie Klingzell	Cory Epler
Courtney Stewart	Craig Olsen
Dalyce Young	Dan Honsberger
Debbie Glick	Devin Schierling
Doug Kinney	Doug Sellers and Conni Briggs
Emilie Smith	Eric Koester
Hannah Moore	Heath and Mikayla Stover
Jaime Minnich	Jake Hammerman
Jamie Guelker	Jamie Libera
Jamie Sheik	Janelle Berry
Jason and Gretchen Haremza	Jason Meysenburg
Jason Newcomer	Jennifer Freeman
Jennifer Clements	Jennifer Gile
Jennifer Miller	Jennifer Thompson

Jenny and Dan Bebout

Jessi Chadd

John Munz

Jordan Roberts

Kaitlin and James Collins

Katie and Seth Stone

Kellen Storer

Kelly Ryan

Kelsie Crist-Funk

Kimberly Bridges

Kristi Richardson

Kyndel Severs

Lindsay Lowe

Lindsey Diercksen

Lisa Patterson

Lucas Bucl

Marcia Klingzell

Mary Dorn

Matt Starkey

Megan Zielonko

Melissa Loerke

Michael McCarthy

Mike Diederich

Molly Simmons

Nifemi Aluko

Patrick and Lauren Amey

Pattie Wolters

Preston and Sarah Schotte

Rosie and JR Bosse

Sally and Casey Irwin

Sarah Baker

Jeremy and Gina Platt

Joan Murry

Joni Lindquist

Julie and Jeff Moore

Kaleb Effland

Katie and Kevin York

Kelly and Mark Perrier

Kelsey Olson

Kim Baldwin

Kimberly Koharchik-Beneke

Kristin Haney

Lauren Hinds

Lindsey Epstein

Lisa and Jake Barge

Lori and TJ Vilkanskas

Marc Shaffer

Marian Kaplan

Mary and Matt Foster

Megan and Gareth Rohr

Melissa Ballard

Melissa Ryan

Michelle Bowen

Mimi Skinner

Natalie Lackey

Pamela Miller and Mike Cummings

Patrick Frank

Paula and Jim Oder

Qianyun Gong

Roxanne Martens

Sam and Wendy Johnson

Sarah and Gary Gibson

Sarah Nelson	Sarah Pfannenstiel
Sarah Stewart	Sascha Fincham
Shannon Glidden	Sharla Meisenheimer
Stephanie and Mike Carlin	Stewart and Joy Koesten
The Sabin Agency	Tiffany and Victor Garza
Tom Russell	Travis and Dakota Tannahill
Tyson Jones	Vickie Dunafon
Weylan Bosse	

To my coworkers at Aspyre Wealth Partners, you all have been amazingly supportive and patient during this insane process. *Thank you!*

A *huge* thank you to the gang at New Degree Press, especially Eric Koester, Anne Kelley, and Miko Marsh, for helping make this dream a reality. Without your help and guidance, this book would still be a "someday" project.

Lastly, thank *you* for buying this book and educating yourself to create a better financial future for you and your family. My goal with this book was to make financial education more accessible to everyone so they can lead the best life possible. You are helping to make that happen.

I am so lucky to have every one of you in my life.

APPENDIX

———

INTRODUCTION

Federal Reserve. Report on the Economic Well-Being of US Households in 2018. Federal Reserve. May 2019. https://www.federalreserve.gov/publications/2019-economic-well-being-of-us-households-in-2018-dealing-with-unexpected-expenses.htm.

Minhaj, Hasan testifying before congress. YouTube. 2019. https://www.youtube.com/watch?v=jfIDh2yGn_g.

National Institute on Retirement Security. "New Research Finds 95 Percent of Millennials Not Saving Adequately for Retirement." February 27, 2018. https://www.nirsonline.org/2018/02/new-research-finds-95-percent-of-millennials-not-saving-adequately-for-retirement.

Pew Research Center. "The Generations Defined." March 1, 2018. https://www.pewresearch.org/st_18-02-27_generations_defined.

Quintero, Ronald. "New payoff study finds nearly 1 in 4 Americans and 1 in 3 Millennials suffer from PTSD-like symptoms caused by financially induced stress." Business Wire. April 20, 2016. https://www.businesswire.com/news/home/20160420005504/en/New-Payoff-Study-Finds-Nearly-1-in-4-Americans-and-1-in-3-Millennials-Suffer-From-PTSD-Like-Symptoms-Caused-by-Financially-Induced-Stress.

Whistle, Wesley. "A Look at Millennial Student Debt." Forbes. October 3, 2019. https://www.forbes.com/sites/wesleywhistle/2019/10/03/a-look-at-millennial-student-debt/?sh=462051092437.

CHAPTER 1

Beaton, Caroline. "We're Wired to Take the Path of Least Resistance". The Gen Y Guide. Psychology Today. March 11, 2017. https://www.psychologytoday.com/us/blog/the-gen-y-guide/201703/were-wired-take-the-path-least-resistance.

Bialik, Kristen and Richard Fry. "Millennial Life: How Young Adulthood Today Compares with Prior Generations." January 30, 2019. https://www.pewresearch.org/social-trends/2019/02/14/millennial-life-how-young-adulthood-today-compares-with-prior-generations-2.

Clear, James. *Atomic Habits: Tiny Changes, Remarkable Results: An Easy and Proven Way to Build Good Habits and Break Bad Ones.* New York. Avery. 2018.

Hamilton, Chad. "Puzzle on the box thing." "I don't know who came up with this analogy originally, but I credit it to a past boss, Chad Hamilton, because it was something he always used to say, and I can never forget it. Thanks Chad!"

Heath, Chip, and Dan Heath. 2011. *Switch: how to change things when change is hard*. Waterville, Me: Thorndike Press.

Kitces, Michael. Interview with Amy Mullen. *Financial Advisor Success Podcast*. Podcast Audio. April 13, 2021.

Klontz, Brad. "The 4 Money Scripts". Journal of Financial Therapy. 2011. https://www.yourmentalwealthadvisors.com/our-process/your-money-script.

Money Scripts Assessment. www.yourmentalwealthadvisors.com.

Money Quotient Website. www.moneyquotient.com. Accessed January 2021.

Richards, Carl. *The Behavior Gap: Simple Ways to Stop Doing Dumb Things with Money*. New York. Portfolio/Penguin. January 2, 2012.

CHAPTER 2

Alvarez, Janet. "Good Debt vs. Bad Debt: Why What You've Been Told is Probably Wrong." CNBC. July 20, 2020. https://www.cnbc.com/2020/07/20/good-debt-vs-bad-debt-why-what-youve-been-told-is-probably-wrong.html

Clark, Biron. "How Long Does It Take to Find a Job?" Career-Sidekick.com. 2020 https://careersidekick.com/average-job-search-time.

Dogen, Sam. "Recommended New Worth Allocation Mix by Age and Work Experience." Financial Samurai. Accessed May 3, 2021. https://www.financialsamurai.com/recommended-net-worth-allocation-mix-by-age-and-work-experience.

Dogen, Sam. "Suggested Net Worth Growth Target Rates by Age". Financial Samurai. Accessed 4/3/2021. https://www.financial-samurai.com/suggested-net-worth-growth-targets-by-age.

Friedberg, Barbara. "Net Worth Goals by Age." The Balance. June 26, 2020. https://www.thebalance.com/net-worth-targets-by-age-4142956.

Indeed Editorial Team. "How Long Does It Take to Find a Job?" Indeed.com. February 22, 2021.

Miles, Karen. "How Much You'll Spend on Childcare." BabyCenter.com. October 15, 2020.

Fernando, Jason. "Time Value of Money." Investopedia.com. Updated February 20, 2021.

Report on the Economic Well-Being of US Households in 2018. May 2019. https://www.federalreserve.gov/publications/2019-economic-well-being-of-us-households-in-2018-dealing-with-unexpected-expenses.htm.

Stanley, Thomas J., William D. Danko, and Cotter Smith. *The Millionaire Next Door*. Prince Frederick, MD: Recorded Books. 2000.

CHAPTER 3

CBN News "1 Out of 3 Americans Don't Use a Budget: But 93% Say Everyone Needs a Budget". May 26, 2019. https://www1.cbn. com/cbnnews/finance/2019/may/1-out-of-3-americans-dont-use-a-budget-but-93-say-everyone-needs-a-budget.

Friedman, Zack. "78% of Workers Live Paycheck to Paycheck." Forbes. January 11, 2019. https://www.forbes.com/sites/zack-friedman/2019/01/11/live-paycheck-to-paycheck-government-shutdown/?sh=2b61f4d84f10.

Glink, Ilyce and Samuel Tamkin. "A Breakdown of What Living Paycheck to Paycheck Looks Like." *The Washington Post*. August 17, 2020. https://www.washingtonpost.com/business/2020/08/17/breakdown-what-living-paycheck-to-paycheck-looks-like.

Kahler, Rick. Foxcraft. "Budgeting with the 3 Bucket System." Financial Awakenings Blog. Accessed January 2021. https:// kahlerfinancial.com/financial-awakenings/weekly-column/budgeting-with-the-bucket-system.

Mint.com "Survey: 65% of American's Have No Idea How Much They Spent Last Month." Updated May 29, 2020. https://mint. intuit.com/blog/budgeting/spending-knowledge-survey/

"Personal Finance Statistics." Debt.com. 2017. https://www.debt.com/statistics.

Ramsey, Dave. "Money, Marriage, and Communication." Ramsey Solutions. April 28, 2021. https://www.daveramsey.com/research/money-marriage-communication.

Ramsey, Dave. "Money Ruining Marriages in America: A Ramsey Solutions Study". February 27, 2018. https://www.daveramsey.com/pr/money-ruining-marriages-in-america.

Schwahn, Lauren. "How to Choose the Right Budget System." Nerdwallet. December 17, 2019. https://www.nerdwallet.com/article/finance/how-to-choose-the-right-budget-system.

Stobierski, Tim "What is a Budget and Why Should I Use One"?" Acorns. September 6, 2019. https://www.acorns.com/money-basics/saving-and-budgeting/budget-meaning/#:~:-text=And%20yet%2C%20only%2041%20percent,your%20finances%20back%20on%20track%3F.

CHAPTER 4

2017 Disability Statistics Annual Report. Institute on Disability/UCED. University of New Hampshire. 2017. https://disability-compendium.org/sites/default/files/user-uploads/2017_Annu-alReport_2017_FINAL.pdf.

Andrasfay, Theresa and Noreen Goldman. Research article—National Academy of Sciences of the United States of America. "Reductions in 2020 US Life Expectancy Due to COVID-19 and the Disproportionate Impact on the Black and Latino Populations." February 2, 2021. https://www.pnas.org/content/118/5/e2014746118. https://www.census.gov/content/dam/Census/library/publications/2020/demo/p25-1145.pdf

Comitz/Beethe Disability Insurance Attorneys. "What is the Difference Between an Own Occupation and Any Occupation Policy?" Accessed March 2021. https://www.disabilitycounsel.net/firm/physician-resources/what-is-the-difference-between-own-occ-and-any-occ/#:~:text=Generally%20speaking%2C%20though%2C%20an%20%E2%80%9C,unable%20to%20work%20in%20any.

Cortland, Pat "Are you part of the middle class? This calculator can tell you." Considerable. December 12, 2020. https://www.considerable.com/money/economy/what-is-middle-class-in-every-state.

Engevik, Jen. "New Survey: 50% of Single Parents Don't Have Life Insurance." April 16, 2019. https://parentology.com/new-survey-50-of-single-parents-dont-have-life-insurance.

Farm Bureau. "4 types of People Who Need Disability Insurance" Farm Bureau Financial Services Website. Accessed March 3, 2020. https://www.fbfs.com/learning-center/4-types-of-people-who-need-disability-insurance.

Lake, Rebecca "Is Group Life Insurance Through Work Enough?" Havenlife blog. September 29, 2020. https://havenlife.com/blog/group-term-life-insurance-through-work.

Moran, Porcshe "How Much is a Stay at Home Parent Worth?" March 21, 2020. https://www.investopedia.com/financial-edge/0112/how-much-is-a-homemaker-worth.aspx.

Simply Insurance. "Average US Life Expectancy Statistics by Gender, Ethnicity, State." 2021. https://www.simplyinsurance.com/average-us-life-expectancy-statistics.

SSA.gov. "The Faces and Facts of Disability." Accessed April 2021. https://www.ssa.gov/disabilityfacts/facts.html#:~:text=The%20sobering%20fact%20for%2020,when%20they%20need%20it%20most.

Ward, Lauren. "Life Insurance for Parents" Bankrate.com February 16, 2021. https://www.bankrate.com/insurance/life-insurance/life-insurance-for-parents.

CHAPTER 5

2021 Wills and Estate Planning Study. Caring.com. Accessed April 2021. https://www.caring.com/caregivers/estate-planning/wills-survey.

Alterman, Elizabeth. Next Avenue/Forbes "How to Find a Good Estate Planner." September 11, 2019. https://www.forbes.com/sites/nextavenue/2019/09/11/how-to-find-a-good-estate-planner/?sh=630596bd2541.

American Academy of Estate Planning Attorneys Website. Accessed February 2021. https://www.aaepa.com/member_directory.

Arias, Elizabeth, Betzaida Tejada-Vera. "Provisional Life Expectancy Estimates for January Through June 2020." NVSS Statistics Rapid Release. February 2021. https://www.cdc.gov/nchs/data/vsrr/VSRR10-508.pdf.

Creative Planning Wills and Trust Center. Accessed May 2021. https://willandtrustcenter.com/wills-trusts-more/probate/#:~:text=Assets%3A%20During%20the%20probate%20process,sell%20assets%20with%20court%20permission.&text=However%2C%20some%20people%20actually%20%E2%80%9Cwork,inherit%20substantial%20sums%20of%20money.

Heirs and Successes. "Steig Larsson's Posthumous Legacy." November 14, 2018. https://heirsandsuccesses.com/2018/11/14/stieg-larssons-posthumous-legacy.

NAEPC National Association of Estate Planners and Councils Website. Accessed February 2021.https://www.naepc.org/designations/estate-planners/search#spec/All.

Smart Money Mamas. "Family Emergency Binder." Smartmoneymamas.com. Accessed May 2021. www.smartmoneymamas.com/ice-binder.

CHAPTER 6

AARP. "Updating Social Security for the 21st Century: 12 Proposals You Should Know About". AARP. October 2015. https://www.aarp.org/work/social-security/info-05-2012/future-of-social-security-proposals.html.

Anspach, Dana. "The "100 Minus Age Rule" Puts Retirees at Risk." The Balance. May 9, 2021. https://www.thebalance.com/100-minus-age-allocation-approach-puts-retirees-at-risk-2388296.

Employee Tenure Summary. US Bureau of Labor Statistics. September 22, 2020. https://www.bls.gov/news.release/tenure.nro.htm.

Eskow, Richard "If You Think Social Security is in Trouble Because We're Living Longer, Look at the Numbers" Blog. September 14, 2010. https://ourfuture.org/20100914/If_You_Think_Social_Securitys_In_Trouble_Because_Were_Living_Longer_Look_At_the_Numbers.

LCV Advisors Blog. "Investing for a Longer Life: Why 120 is the new 100." August 15, 2018. https://lcvadvisors.com/blog/investing-for-a-longer-life-why-120-is-the-new-100#:~:text=-For%20many%20years%2C%20a%20widely,of%20their%20holding%20in%20stocks.

Sethi, Ramit. *I Will Teach You to Be Rich* (Second Edition). New York: Workman Publishing. 2019.

Sokunbi, Bola. *Grow Your Money*. New Jersey: John Wiley & Sons, Inc. 2020.

CHAPTER 7

Backman, Maurie. "43% of Millennials are Making This Major Money Mistake". The Motley Fool. June 8, 2019. https://www.

fool.com/retirement/2019/07/08/43-of-millennials-are-making-this-major-money-mist.aspx.

Doyle, Karen "43% of Millennials Aren't Investing—and that's a Problem" Yahoo News. June 27, 2019. https://news.yahoo.com/43-millennials-aren-t-investing-090000387.html.

Fidelity FMRCo. Research Team. March 2020. https://www.fidelity.com/bin-public/060_www_fidelity_com/documents/dont-miss-best-days.pdf.

Fidelity Investment Strategy Report. 2020. https://www.fidelity.com/bin-public/060_www_fidelity_com/documents/wealth-planning_investment-strategy.pdf.

Imbert, Fred "Stocks Post Best Annual Gain in 6 Years with the S&P 500 Surging More Than 28%" CNBC December 31, 2019. https://www.cnbc.com/2019/12/31/dow-futures-last-trading-day-of-2019.html.

Jason, Julie JD, LLM "The Coronavirus Stock Market: A Market Gone Wild". Forbes Magazine. April 8, 2020. https://www.forbes.com/sites/juliejason/2020/04/08/the-coronavirus-stock-market-a-market-gone-wild/?sh=62087e3fa31f.

Lenihan, Rob "Dow and S&P 500 Close at Records on Last Trading Day of 2020." The Street. December 31, 2020. https://www.thestreet.com/investing/stocks-waver-on-last-trading-day-of-2020.

Speights, Keith "S&P 500 Index Fund Average Annual Return." The Motley Fool. May 15, 2021. https://www.fool.com/invest-

ing/2018/02/08/heres-what-a-10000-investment-in-an-sp-500-
index-f.aspx.

CHAPTER 8

Anthony, James. "98 Trade School vs College Statistics in 2020/2021: Education Cost and Job Outlook Analysis". FinancesOnline. Accessed May 2021. https://financesonline.com/trade-school-college-statistics.

Carnevale, Anthony P., and Ben Cheah. "Five Rules of the College and Career Game". Georgetown University Center of Education and the Workforce. 2018. https://1gyh0q479ufd3yna29x7u-bjn-wpengine.netdna-ssl.com/wp-content/uploads/Fiverules.pdf.

CollegeFinance Blog. "Trade School vs. College Degree Salaries: Who Makes More?" Updated May 29, 2020. https://collegefinance.com/plan/trade-school-vs-college-degree-salaries-who-makes-more.

Florida National University. "Why a college degree can mean a higher paying job." July 9, 2019. https://www.fnu.edu/college-degree-higher-paying-job/#:~:text=According%20to%20the%20U.S.%20Bureau,not%20to%20pursue%20a%20diploma.

Foxcraft. "Give Kids the Gift of College Success". Kahler Financial Group Blog. Accessed April 2021. https://kahlerfinancial.com/financial-awakenings/weekly-column/give-kids-the-gift-of-college-success.

Hanson, Melanie. "How do People Pay for College?" Educationdata. org. April 15, 2021. https://educationdata.org/how-do-people-pay-for-college#:~:text=76.7%25%20of%20full%2Dtime%20 undergraduates,from%20private%20or%20community%20 organizations.

Hamm, Trent. "Trade school might be a better choice than college. Here's why." Lifehacker. December 16, 2019. https://lifehacker. com/trade-school-might-be-a-better-choice-than-college-her-1484086007#:~:text=For%20starters%2C%20the%20salary%20 isn,college%20graduate%20is%20only%20%2490%2C000.

Hanson, Melanie. "Average Cost of College and Tuition." Educationdata.org. May 14, 2021. https://educationdata.org/average-cost-of-college.

Kobliner, Beth. "Have you had the College Talk?" bethkobliner. com. Accessed March 2021. https://bethkobliner.com/guides/ we-need-to-talk-college/start-college-conversation/initial-college-talk/#:~:text=And%20for%20that%20reason%2C%20 it,your%20kid%20might%20be%20experiencing.

Rockford Career College Blog. "8 Benefits of Going to Trade School". April 26, 2016. https://www.rockfordcareercollege. edu/blog/8-benefits-going-trade-school.

Webber, Douglas. "Is College worth it? Going Beyond the Averages." Third Way Report. September 18, 2018. https://www.thirdway. org/report/is-college-worth-it-going-beyond-averages#:~:text=A%20college%20degree%20has%20substantial,is%20not%20 without%20risk%2C%20however.

CHAPTER 9

Asebedo, Sarah, and Martin Seay. "From Functioning to Flourishing: Applying Positive Psychology to Financial Planning." Journal of Financial Planning 28 (11): 50–58. 2015.

Brennan, Rosemary. "5 Things You Need to Know About Money and Relationships." Glamour. August 2, 2010. https://www.glamour.com/story/5-things-you-need-to-know-abou-2010-08.

Brigham Young University. "Stop Thinking Your Wife is Bad with Money." Science Daily. August 16, 2017. https://www.sciencedaily.com/releases/2017/08/170816112655.htm.

Britt-Lutter, Sonya, Camila Haselwood & Emily Koochel. "Love and Money: Reducing Stress and Improving Couple Happiness." Marriage & Family Review 55:4, 330–345. 2019.

Ellis, Laura. "How Early 'Money Memories' Shape Our Choices for Life." Money Memories Podcast. January 20, 2021. https://wfpl.org/new-podcast-how-early-money-memories-shape-our-choices-for-life.

Hamid Rao, Aliya. "Even Breadwinning Wives Don't Get Equality at Home." *The Atlantic*. May 12, 2019. https://www.theatlantic.com/family/archive/2019/05/breadwinning-wives-gender-inequality/589237.

Hill, Catey. "This Common Behavior is the No. 1 Predictor of Whether You Will Get Divorced." MarketWatch. January 10, 2018. https://www.marketwatch.com/story/this-common-

behavior-is-the-no-1-predictor-of-whether-youll-get-di-
vorced-2018-01-10.

Horch, AJ. "How to Better Understand Your Partner's 'Money
Personality'." CNBC. November 24, 2020. https://www.
cnbc.com/2020/11/23/how-to-better-understand-your-part-
ners-money-personality.html.

Kahler, Rick. "Spender or Saver: What Spouses See vs. What They
Do." Financial Awakenings Blog. Accessed March 2021. https://
kahlerfinancial.com/financial-awakenings/money-psychology/
spender-or-saver-what-spouses-see-vs-what-they-do.

Krauss Whitbourne, Susan. "5 Stressless Ways to Talk to Your
Partner About Money." Psychology Today. July 20, 2019.
https://www.psychologytoday.com/us/blog/fulfillment-any-
age/201907/5-stressless-ways-talk-your-partner-about-money.

Leonhardt, Megan. "75% of Millennial Couples Talk About Money
at Least Once a Week—and it Seems to Be Working for Them."
CNBC. July 27, 2018. https://www.cnbc.com/2018/07/27/75-per-
cent-of-millennial-couples-talk-about-money-at-least-once-a-
week.html.

Leonhardt, Megan. "Americans Would Rather Talk About Anything Other than how Much Money They Make, Even Politics."
CNBC. August 9, 2018. https://www.cnbc.com/2018/08/08/
americans-would-rather-talk-about-anything-than-income.
html.

Rodsky, Eve. "I Created a System to Make Sure My Husband and I
Divide Household Duties Fairly. Here's How it Works." Time.

October 1, 2019. https://time.com/5690007/divide-household-chores-fairly.

Thakor, Manisha *"Get Financially Naked. How to Talk Money with your Honey."* Adams Media. 2009.

CHAPTER 10

Carseatresearch.com. "How Much Does a Car Seat Cost?" Accessed April 2021.

Chapkanovska, Evangelina. "How Much Does It Cost to Raise a Child?" SpendMeNot. May 20, 2021. https://spendmenot.com/blog/how-much-does-it-cost-to-raise-a-child/#:~:text=The%20cost%20of%20raising%20a,the%20Urban%20West%20is%20%24245%2C460.

CostHelper Children Inc. "How Much Does a Stroller Cost?" Accessed March 2021. https://children.costhelper.com/strollers.html#:~:text=Typical%20costs%3A,can%20cost%20more%20than%20%24700.

Daly, Lyle. "Personal Bankruptcy Statistics for 2020". The Ascent. March 24, 2020. https://www.fool.com/the-ascent/research/personal-bankruptcy-statistics.

Friedman, Zack. "78% of Workers live paycheck to paycheck". Forbes. January 11, 2019. https://www.forbes.com/sites/zack-friedman/2019/01/11/live-paycheck-to-paycheck-government-shutdown/?sh=238482224f10.

Lino, Mark. "The Cost of Raising a Child." US Department of Agriculture. February 18, 2020.

CHAPTER 11

Godfrey, Joline. *Raising Financially Fit Kids.* Berkeley, California. Ten Speed Press. 2013.

Godfrey, Neale S. *Money Doesn't Grow on Trees: A Parent's Guide to Raising Financially Responsible Children.* United States. Atria Books. 2006.

Goudreau, Jenna. "Nearly 60% of Parents provide financial support to adult children". Forbes. May 20, 2011. https://www.forbes.com/sites/jennagoudreau/2011/05/20/parents-provide-financial-support-money-adult-children/?sh=568d49e91987.

Lahey, Jessica. *The Gift of Failure.* United States. Harper Collins. 2015.

Lieber, Ron. *The Opposite of Spoiled.* New York. Harper. 2016, 2015

"Money as You Grow: Help for Parents and Caregivers". Consumer Financial Protection Bureau. Accessed 2018.

Ramsey, Dave and Rachel Cruze. *Smart Money Smart Kids.* Nashville, Tennessee. Thomas Nelson Publishers. 2014.